The Parent Playbooks

2nd Edition
Fun and Enjoyable Learning Activities with Kids

GRADES 6 - 8

Standards-Based Learning Activities

- Parent-Teacher tested
- Parent-Teacher contributed
- Fun ways to learn new ideas and apply old ones

Dr. Joni Samples

The Parent Playbooks: Grades 6 - 8

Printed and bound in the United States of America

ENGAGE! Press
2485 Norte Dame Blvd 370-170
Chico,CA 95928
www.engagepress.com

First Printing 2019
ISBN No. 978-0-9906335-4-9
Library of Congress Cataloging–in–Publication Data

DEDICATION

The Parent Playbook series is dedicated to the memory of Linda Armstrong. Linda was a lover of books and literature, a librarian and writer, my editor and keeper of databases, believer in families and learning, and, above all, my friend.

ABOUT YOUR PARENT PLAYBOOK

Dear Parents,

Welcome to the Parent Playbook series, where you will find recipes for learning. Similar to a cookbook, each activity begins with a list of needed materials, the time required to complete the activity, and a description of the activity. Instead of a "daily nutritional requirement," these recipes relate to State Educational Standards for learning. The activities are easy and fun.

I am a lifelong educator with four children. During my child rearing days, my cooking rarely came from a cookbook. Meal planning consisted of whatever I could recall from my childhood or what would heat up quickly in the microwave.

My interest in assisting my children in education focused on, like my menu for meals, something quick, easy, and able to make a positive difference in a fun way. However, there was nothing available on the market that gave me easy directions and ideas to help my children become successful learners. I dredged stuff up from my teaching days or depended on their schools to provide something. But, homework didn't entertain me or my children enough to do more than what was due the next day. We would lose interest, so I began creating other activities to do.

It was then that my husband suggested that I write a column in the newspaper to share the activities with other parents. As the newly elected County Superintendent of Schools in our area and someone who wanted to let folks know I was on the job, that sounded like a winning idea. I could provide teachers, parents, and myself with home activities that were easy, fun and enhanced learning.

One day a colleague remarked, "That muffin activity sure did a lot of measuring of fractions. Which grade level standard is that?" Of course! Share activities and match them to the learning standards taught in the classroom and everyone wins. With that the idea for the Parent Playbooks was born.

Parents enjoy a fun learning time with their children. The activities they do together reinforce concepts taught at school. The teachers see the support from home reflected in the children's schoolwork. In addition, the kids — their grades, test scores and self-confidence are off the charts. So, here you have recipes for learning in the form of Parent Playbooks.

Taste, benefit from, and most of all experience the delicious joy of learning with your children.

Sincerely,
Dr. Joni

A Letter from Dr. Joni and Trinidad:

To the Kids

Trinidad says hi and welcome to The Parent Playbooks — a place where learning is fun!

You might think Trinidad learns mostly at the beach, but this is one starfish that gets around town. Grocery stores, movies, pizza parlors, and the library are just a few of the spots Trinidad is likely to show up. See how often you can find Trinidad as you and your family learn through the activities shared in this book. Don't forget to create your own activities. There is plenty of room for you and your family to write in the "What We Learned Today" section.

Enjoy the activities along with Trinidad and Make Learning Fun!

Sincerely,

Dr. Joni and Trinidad

Table of Contents

For workshops or presentations by Dr. Joni, contact Family Friendly Schools:

Phone/Fax: 1-530-899-8423
www.familyfriendlyschools.com

ABOUT THE LEARNING STANDARDS

The standards used in the Parent Playbook series are a combination of Common Core Standards for English Language Arts and Math.

The standards used in this material are a representation of all state learning standards, and are tested in every state.

The major purpose for use of the standards is to provide teachers and parents a guideline for skills taught at each grade level.

Standards for Science and Social Studies are tested in every state. Science and Social Studies activities for parents are included here and matched to a set of standards derived from standards from across the United States.

We do hope these activities will be both enjoyable and filled with learning for both parents, teachers, and, most important, children.

ENGLISH LANGUAGE ARTS

6 – 8

Parent Playbook Activities

Want to add your favorite activity to the next Parent Playbook?
Use the convenient form in the back of this book or contact the publisher at:

www.familyfriendlyschools.com • www.engagepress.com

By Dr. Joni Samples **English Language Arts Learning Standards**

ENGLISH LANGUAGE ARTS LEARNING STANDARDS
Grades 6-8

The purpose for English Language Arts (ELA) Standards is to guarantee that all students develop the language skills they need to succeed in life as informed, productive members of society.

The ability to read and write begins before children enter school as they experience and experiment with language activities – from babbling to learning sounds and words.

Children begin to make connections between reading, writing, speaking, and listening as a way of gathering information and learning about the world around them.

The ELA Standards are listed on the following page to help you understand and put together all the skills needed to read and write. No standard stands alone. They all work together to create a language arts program.

Basic Topics of the English Language Arts Learning Standards Grades 6-8

Reading Standards for Literature
- Key Ideas and Details
- Craft and Structure
- Integration of Knowledge and Ideas
- Range of Reading and Level of Text Complexity

Reading Standards for Informational Text
- Key Ideas and Details
- Craft and Structure
- Integration of Knowledge and Ideas
- Range of Reading and Level of Text Complexity

Reading Standards Foundational Skills
- Phonics and Word Recognition
- Fluency

Writing Standard
- Text Types and Purposes
- Production and Distribution of Writing
- Research to Build and Present Knowledge
- Range of Writing

Speaking and Listening Standard
- Comprehension and Collaboration
- Presentation and Knowledge of Ideas

Language Standard
- Conventions of Standard English
- Knowledge of Language
- Vocabulary Acquisition and Use

Aesop's Fables

Number of People: 2 Time: 30 minutes

Grade Level 

Materials: Aesop's Fables

Description: Aesop, an ancient Greek, told animal stories with a moral. They are called fables. One favorite is *The Tortoise and the Hare*. Let your child choose one or more of Aesop's fables. After reading the story, let your child write his own moral to the story in more modern day terms.

ENGLISH LANGUAGE ARTS STANDARD

Reading Standards for Literature: Key Ideas and Details

1. Cite textual evidence to support analysis of what the text says explicitly as well as inferences drawn from the text.

Book List

Number of People: 2 Time: A few minutes

Grade Level 

Materials: Card file, notebook or computer list

Description: Having your child write book reports is one way of keeping track of what he reads. Another is having your child keep a card file, notebook, or list of the books he has read on his computer. His list will give you ideas of what he likes to read. Book interest lists help when he is trying to figure out what to write a report on or has a speech to prepare.

ENGLISH LANGUAGE ARTS STANDARD

Reading standards for Literature: Key Ideas and Details

2. Determine a theme or central idea of a text and how it is conveyed through particular details; provide a summary of the text distinct from personal opinions or judgments.

STARfish could show up in a tent on the beach!

Reading Time

Number of People: 2+ Time: Varies

Grade Level 

Materials: Reading materials

Description: Here are some ideas for making reading a story a fun activity:

1. On Friday or Saturday plan a late bedtime so your children can read before they go to sleep.
2. On a rainy night provide everyone with flashlights and let the children read for an hour.
3. One night a week at dinner, have your child share a story he or she is reading.
4. Set up a tent outside just for quiet reading time.

ENGLISH LANGUAGE ARTS STANDARD

Reading Standards for Literature: Integration of Knowledge and Ideas

7. Compare and contrast the experience of reading a story, drama, or poem to listening to or viewing an audio, video, or live version of the text, including contrasting what they "see" and "hear" when reading the text to what they perceive when they listen or watch.

What we learned today...

____

____

____

____

____

____

____

Author, Author

Number of People: 2 Time: Varies

Grade Level 

Materials: Paper and pencil, books, library, or the Internet

Description: *Harry Potter and the Sorcerer's Stone* was written by J. K. Rowling. Have your children identify their favorite fiction books. Have them name as many as possible. Then ask them if they know the authors. Do some research to find the names and backgrounds of the authors on her list. After each author, have them note the type of fiction they write and the major characteristics of their form of fiction. Talk about how their favorite author creates the characters and develops the story through the characters.

ENGLISH LANGUAGE ARTS STANDARD

Reading Standards for Literature: Craft and Structure

8. Explain how an author develops the point of view of the narrator or speaker in a text.

What we learned today...

Book Time

Number of People: 2 Time: Varies

Grade Level 

Materials: Books, bookcase materials

Description: If you have a library or a collection of books in your house, expand it. If you don't have one, start one. Bookcases can be bought or made inexpensively. A few bricks and a couple of boards will get you started. Let your child arrange the books the way he wants. Keep adding to his collection on a regular basis. Let him match his selections to his interests and grade level.

ENGLISH LANGUAGE ARTS STANDARD

Reading Standards for Literature: Integration of Knowledge and Ideas

9. Compare and contrast texts in different forms or genres in terms of their approaches to similar themes and topics.

SSR (Sustained Silent Reading)

Number of People: 2+ Time: 15-30 minutes

Grade Level 

Materials: Books, magazines, or other reading material

Description: Schools have what they call SSR — Sustained Silent Reading. It's a designated time in the school day when everyone in the school reads. This includes students, teachers, secretaries, principal – everyone. You can do the same thing at home. Pick a time when the TV, radio, CDs and the phones are turned off, and everyone reads including Mom and Dad. Reading can be from books, magazines, or the newspaper, but everyone reads. Thirty minutes or more is a good length of time for scheduled reading. Anyone can choose to read longer, but everyone reads for at least the designated time period.

ENGLISH LANGUAGE ARTS STANDARD

Reading Standards for Literature: Range of Reading and Level of Text Complexity

10. By the end of the year, read and comprehend literature, including stories, dramas, and poems, in the 6-8 text complexity band proficiently, with scaffolding as needed at the high end of the range.

Food Network Star

Grade Level 

Number of People: 2 Time: 30 minutes

Materials: Cookbook or favorite recipe

Description: Have your child choose a recipe he would like to create. He might focus on a meat dish, a casserole, or creating some other kitchen delight. Make a list of needed ingredients, shop, and begin cooking. Discuss any ingredients, terms, or descriptions that are new or different. The "proof of the pudding" is the finished product and satisfied family members.

ENGLISH LANGUAGE ARTS STANDARD

Reading Standards for Informational Text: Craft and Structure

4. Determine the meaning of words and phrases as they are used in a text, including figurative, connotative, and technical meanings.

Refrigerator Words

Grade Level 

Number of People: 1+ Time: 10 minutes

Materials: Magnetic words

Description: Magnetic words on the refrigerator allow your sixth grader to create fun sentences, write poetry, or send a message. See what message he can come up with to influence dinner choices, bedtime, or what to watch on TV. Make sure he has good reasons for his message.

ENGLISH LANGUAGE ARTS STANDARD

Writing Standards: Text Types and Purposes

1. Write arguments to support claims with clear reasons and relevant evidence.

Scrapbooking

Number of People: 1-2 Time: Varies

Grade Level **6**

Materials: Blank Scrapbook, pictures, photos, paper, scissors

Description: Having a scrapbook is all the rage these days. Now that he is entering Junior High, let your child start his own scrapbook. Let him choose his own subject—animals, sports, celebrities, monthly activities, or whatever his interests. Scrapbook interests make for great writing topics. Have your child label the items in the scrapbook then write several paragraphs or a story about each picture.

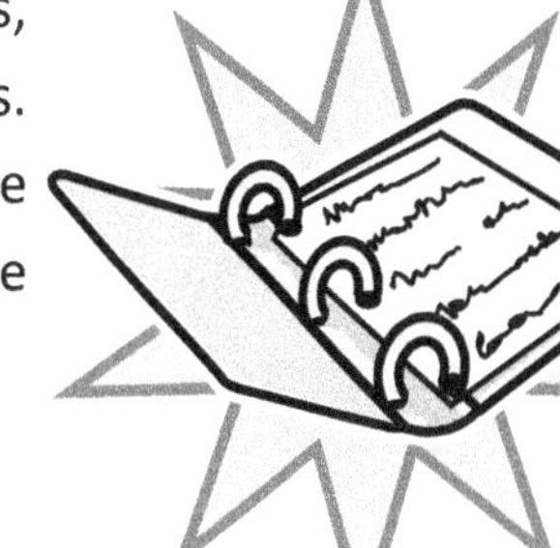

ENGLISH LANGUAGE ARTS STANDARD

Writing Standards: Text Types and Purposes

2. Write informative/explanatory texts to examine a topic and convey ideas, concepts, and information through the selections, organization, and analysis of relevant content.

What we learned today...

Trip Journal

Number of People: 2 Time: 15 minutes

Grade Level **6**

Materials: Paper or a notebook and pencil

Description: Suggest your child keep a journal while on vacation. Where did you have breakfast? What time did you get to the restaurant? Which one? What did you eat? Was it good? What did it cost? Where did you travel for the day? What was the best part of the day? What did you learn about the area we visited? A lot happens on vacations. Have him write it down in his own way as soon after an activity happens as possible. Details are easy to forget and motivations wane, so write soon and enjoy.

ENGLISH LANGUAGE ARTS STANDARD

Writing Standard: Text Types and Purpose

2. Write informative/explanatory texts to examine a topic and convey ideas, concepts, and information through the selection, organization, and analysis of relevant content.

   B. Introduce a topic; organize ideas, concepts, and information, using strategies such as definition, classification, comparison/ contrast, and cause/effect; include formatting, graphics, and multimedia when useful to aiding comprehension.

What we learned today...

Thank You Notes

Number of People: 2+ Time: 20 minutes

Grade Level 

Materials: Thank you notes and pen

Description: Kids love gifts. Any excuse to get a gift will do—birthdays, Christmas, Easter, and Valentine's Day. It doesn't matter. Have them write thank-you notes for those presents. You can insist the thank-you notes say a bit more than, "Thank you for the present, Love Sam." Make the note personal, but be sure it includes content that provides lots of information about what they are planning to do with the gift.

ENGLISH LANGUAGE ARTS STANDARD

Writing Standards: Production and Distribution of Writing

4. Produce clear and coherent writing in which the development, organization, and style are appropriate to task, purpose and audience.

Note This

Number of People: 2 Time: 15 minutes

Grade Level 6

Materials: Paper and pencil or emails

Description: Have your child write letters, *What we learned today...*, and emails. Look over what she has written since creative spelling and punctuation have become common, especially with emails. Make sure the spelling and punctuation is correct.

ENGLISH LANGUAGE ARTS STANDARD

Writing Standards: Production and Distribution of Writing

4. Produce clear and coherent writing in which the development organization, and style are appropriate to task purpose, and audience.

E-mail Writing

Number of People: 2 Time: 15 minutes

Grade Level **6**

Materials: Computer with e-mail

Description: Writing e-mails to friends can be good writing practice, but check the letters before they go out. Chat-type writing tends to get sloppy.

ENGLISH LANGUAGE ARTS STANDARD

Writing Standards: Production and Distribution of Writing

6. With some guidance and support from peers and adults, develop and strengthen writing as needed by planning revising, editing, rewriting, or trying a new approach.

Family Newsletter

Number of People: 2+ Time: Varies

Grade Level **6**

Materials: Computer with newsletter program

Description: Creating a family newsletter is easy when you have a publishing program on your computer. Everyone in the family can write or dictate a story about something they're doing. I have one child who likes to edit and add pictures. Make it fun and something to share with other members of the family.

ENGLISH LANGUAGE ARTS STANDARD

Writing Standard: Production and Distribution of Writing

6. Use technology, including the Internet, to produce and publish writing as well as to interact and collaborate with others; demonstrate sufficient command of keyboarding skills to type a minimum of three pages in a single sitting.

Start Up for Writing

Number of People: 2 Time: 20 minutes

Grade Level 

Materials: Paper and pencil, or computer

Description: It can be challenging at times to start a research writing assignment. You can help your child get started. First, take ten minutes to write down as many possible topics as you can. Make them crazy, silly, or serious, but keep writing for at least ten minutes. When you have finished, have him narrow the topics down to his favorite one. Next, identify the places where he can get information he will need—from books, magazines, or the Internet. Then let him write a rough draft of the paper. Be sure you read it and make comments that will help him stay focused and eventually finish.

ENGLISH LANGUAGE ARTS STANDARD

Writing Standard: Research to Build and Present Knowledge

7. Conduct short research projects to answer a question, drawing on several sources and refocusing the inquiry when appropriate.

What we learned today...

Giveaways

Number of People: 2 Time: 30 minutes

Grade Level 

Materials: Magazine or newspaper, paper and pencil or computer, envelope, stamp

Description: Magazines and newsletters often have items to give away free. Help your child write letters requesting items of interest from those publications. Make sure he writes the letters well enough to persuade the magazine to give him his requested item. Then, address the envelope together the first few times. It takes some time to get the addresses and the stamp in the right place.

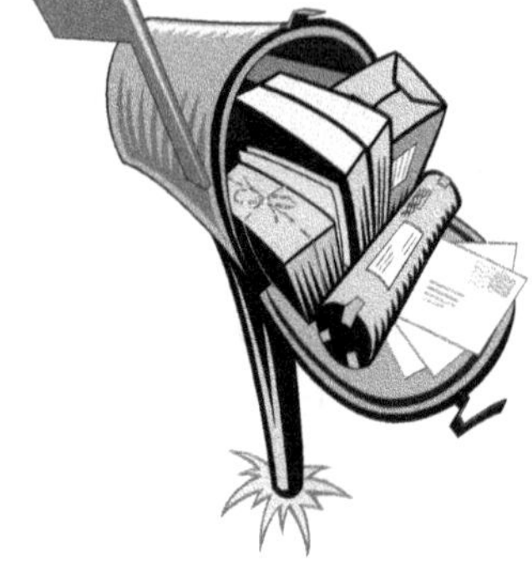

ENGLISH LANGUAGE ARTS STANDARD

Writing Standard: Research to Build and Present Knowledge

8. Gather relevant information from multiple print and digital sources; assess the credibility of each source; and quote or paraphrase the data and conclusions of others while avoiding plagiarism and providing basic bibliographic information for sources.

What we learned today...

Ad Game

Number of People: 2 Time: 20 minutes

Grade Level 

Materials: Writing assignments

Description: Ads are everywhere so on a trip around town or through the grocery aisle, play an ad game. Have one person pick an ad and try to convince the other person why this is the best thing on the market. Be sure to explain all the values and wonderfulness of the product. The other person then gets to explain why they would or wouldn't buy the product based on the presentation.

ENGLISH LANGUAGE ARTS STANDARD

Speaking and Listening Standards: Comprehension and Collaboration

2. Interpret information presented in diverse media and formats and explain how it contributes to a topic, text, or issue under study.

Word Pairs

Number of People: 2 Time: 30 minutes

Grade Level 6

Materials: Paper and pencil, dictionary

Description: See how many word pairs your child can find; one with double consonants and another just like it with the same root word, but only a single consonant. Examples are hopping and hoping, starring and staring, ragged and raged. Ask if they have the same meaning. How many more can he find?

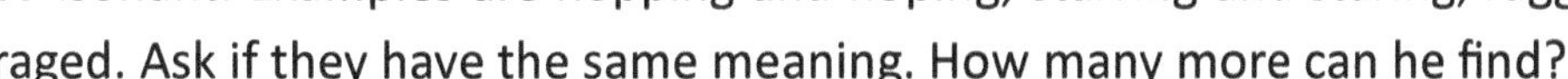

ENGLISH LANGUAGE ARTS STANDARD

Language Standard: Conventions of Standard English

2. Demonstrate command of the conventions of standard English capitalization, punctuation, and spelling when writing.

   B. Spell correctly

Crossword Logic

Number of People: 2+ Time: Varies

Grade Level 

Materials: Crossword puzzle books, pencil

Description: Crossword puzzle books are a great way to build a vocabulary. I like some of the more challenging puzzle-type activities in crossword puzzle books to help with thinking and logic skills. Keep a couple books around the house and make them available for your kids. They're also good on vacation trips when you're in the car for a long time. If someone is stuck on a word, he or she can get suggestions from the rest of the family.

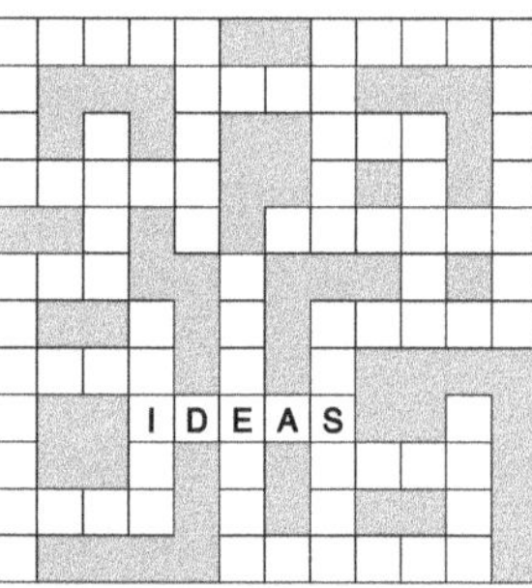

ENGLISH LANGUAGE ARTS STANDARD

Language Standard: Conventions of Standard English

2. Demonstrate command of the conventions of standard English capitalization, punctuation, and spelling when writing.

    B. Spell correctly

Book Travel Reading

Number of People: 1 Time: Varies

Grade Level 

Materials: Magazine and books

Description: Keep books in your car for your child to read while the two of you run errands. My children don't always like to join me in the grocery store. They would rather sit outside and read while I run into the store. This is not true when we get to the mall. Then, they would rather I sit outside while they go shop and visit with their friends. Enjoy talking to them about what they've read while driving home. Have them provide details to support their comments.

ENGLISH LANGUAGE ARTS STANDARD

Reading: Literature: Key Ideas and Details

1. Cite several pieces of textual evidence to support analysis of what the text says explicitly as well as inferences drawn from the text.

I wonder if Tom or Huck ever found STARfish on the Mississippi River?

Favorite Books

Number of People: 2 Time: 15 minutes

Grade Level **7**

Materials: Favorite Book

Description:Some of the favorite books for middle school are *Little Women, The Adventures of Tom Sawyer,* or *Dragonwings.* A favorite poem is "The Road not Taken." Any of these will provide opportunities for the events to unfold and for you and your child to talk about how those events unfold. How does the way the story or poem is written help those events to happen? How long do you wait to find out if Tom and Becky get out of the cave?

ENGLISH LANGUAGE ARTS STANDARD

Reading: Literature

5. Analyze how a drama's or poem's form or structure contributes to its meaning.

What we learned today...

Library Day

Number of People: 2 Time: Day//Week

Grade Level **7**

Materials: Library

Description: Library time is fun time. Consider taking your child to the library each week to check out books, read magazines, research topics of interest or study for a test. Make library time a fun, family habit.

ENGLISH LANGUAGE ARTS STANDARD

Reading: Literature: Range of Reading and Level of Text Complexity.

10. By the end of the year, read and comprehend literature, including stories, dramas, and poems, in the grade 6-8 text complexity band proficiently, with scaffolding as needed at the high end of the range.

What we learned today...

Games

Number of People: 2-4 Time: Several Hours

Grade Level **7**

Materials: Games

Description: Playing games is fun for the whole family. *Trivial Pursuit* and *Brain Quest* are great games and lots of fun. Games also require reading and thinking while providing an evening's entertainment. Look at the games on the shelf at your local toy store and choose ones you think your family will like.

ENGLISH LANGUAGE ARTS STANDARD

Reading: Informational Text

4. Determine the meaning of words and phrases as they are used in a text, including figurative, connotative, and technical meanings; analyze the impact of a specific word choice on meaning and tone.

Computer Notes

Number of People: 2 Time: 10 minutes

Grade Level **7**

Materials: Computer

Description: When I worked at my computer, I wrote reminders to my kids instead of nagging. Computers have stick-it type notes—a sort of text message on the computer. Send a note. If you don't have stick-it notes, send your child an e-mail or text message. Kids like to read something new and different, and it's always fun to get mail in any form.

ENGLISH LANGUAGE ARTS STANDARD

Information Text: Craft and Structure

4. Determine the meaning of words and phrases as they are used in a text, including figurative, connotative, and technical meanings; analyze the impact of a specific word choice on meaning and tone.

Heroes Read

Number of People: 2 Time: 20 minutes

Grade Level **7**

Materials: TV shows or movies

Description: Television shows or movies often show situations in which the hero must read an important technical document, data, or e-mail in order to succeed. Talk about what the main character is reading, and how it helped the character be successful.

ENGLISH LANGUAGE ARTS STANDARD

Reading: Informational Text: Integration of Knowledge and Ideas

8. Trace and evaluate the argument and specific claims in a text, assessing whether the reasoning is sound and the evidence is relevant and sufficient to support the claims.

Subscribe To It

Number of People: 1 Time: Varies

Grade Level **7**

Materials: Magazine subscription

Description: A great birthday present is a subscription to a magazine about something your child likes. One of my children loved baseball and another wanted to know the latest on film and TV stars. Let him read a couple of articles about his favorite topic and discuss what he finds from the different readings. The key is to make sure the topic is something you know he will be interested in reading.

ENGLISH LANGUAGE ARTS STANDARD

Reading: Informational Text

9. Analyze how two or more authors writing about the same topic shape their presentations of key information by emphasizing different evidence or advancing different interpretations of facts.

Try writing a report on STARfish.
We're a great topic to study.

Report Time

Number of People: 2 Time: 30 minutes+

Grade Level **7**

Materials: Paper and pencil or computer

Description: Most of us write reports of one kind or another. Sometimes we write them for work; sometimes we collect information to write a tax report. We write reports for any number of reasons. Our kids in the middle grades will be required to write a number of reports as well. Have your child write his report while you write yours. He can check a paragraph of yours while you check a paragraph of his. Talk about where you found your information and how you word what you want to say about that information. Remember, organized thoughts are important and neatness counts.

ENGLISH LANGUAGE ARTS STANDARD

Writing: Text Types and Purposes

1. Write arguments to support claims with clear reasons and relevant evidence.

What we learned today...

Who STARS in your favorite TV show?

Favorite Character Stories

Number of People: 2 Time: Varies

Grade Level **7**

Materials: Paper and pencil or computer

Description: Who are your teen's favorite characters in books or on TV? Have him write his own story featuring one of those favorite characters. Jack (*Law and Order*) can prosecute someone from the football team who he believes stole the team's mascot. Harry (*Harry Potter*) can visit school for a day and uncover the math teacher's secret wizardry. You can help edit the first draft. Encourage him to write stories and get his ideas on paper. He can clean them up later.

ENGLISH LANGUAGE ARTS STANDARD

Writing: Text types and Purposes

3. Write narratives to develop real or imagined experiences or events using effective technique, relevant descriptive details, and well-structured event sequences.

What we learned today...

First Draft

Number of People: 2 Time: 30 minutes

Grade Level **7**

Materials: Paper and pencil or computer

Description: Have your child write his first draft of a writing assignment. Go over it together paying special attention to how well he has done. Major errors need to be pointed out, but you don't need to go heavy with a red pen. Ask clarifying questions so he can think through what he wants to say. Remind him that most authors go through many drafts.

ENGLISH LANGUAGE ARTS STANDARD

Writing: Production and distribution of Writing

4. Produce clear and coherent writing in which the development, organization, and style are appropriate to task, purpose, and audience.

Topical Ideas

Number of People: 2 Time: Varies

Grade Level **7**

Materials: Paper and pencil or computer for writing

Description: Your middle school student is going to do a good deal of writing. Help your child gather topics for writing activities. A child needs topics. Great experiences make for great writing topics. Take him to places where he can gain experiences and research his topics—aquariums, zoos, museums, vacation spots or just a walk around town. Give him experiences at home to write about too. Let him build a cabinet, bake bread from scratch, or learn to play the drums. All are writable activities.

ENGLISH LANGUAGE ARTS STANDARD

Writing: Research to Build and Present Knowledge

8. Gather relevant information from multiple print and digital sources, using search terms effectively, asses the credibility and accuracy of each source, and quote or paraphrase the data and conclusions of others while avoiding plagiarism and following a standard format for citation.

Letter to the Editor

Number of People: 2 Time: Varies

Grade Level **7**

Materials: Newspaper

Description: Have your child do a bit of research about events in your community. Have him read the newspaper for a week and listen to news stories. Let him keep a chart of the various kinds of events that are reported. Have him visit the police station and ask about the events for the week. Ask him to form an opinion about a community event and how they are being reported in the media. Have him write a letter to the editor with his opinion.

ENGLISH LANGUAGE ARTS STANDARD

Writing: Research to Build and Present Knowledge

8. Gather relevant information from multiple print and digital sources, using search terms effectively; assess the credibility and accuracy of each source; and quote or paraphrase the data and conclusions of others while avoiding plagiarism and following a standard format for citation.

Listening to the News

Number of People: 1+ Time: 20 minutes

Grade Level **7**

Materials: Paper and pencil or computer

Description: CNN, Fox, or any news report often features stories claiming to be factual. If you listen to the same story on two channels, it may be different. Have your child choose a story he likes. Have him listen to it or read about it in several different media presentations. Ask him to get details from the different sources then explain what he has found. My son liked to come up with stories about why his favorite ballplayer should or should not be in the hall of fame.

ENGLISH LANGUAGE ARTS STANDARD

Speaking & Listening: Comprehension and Collaboration

2. Analyze the main ideas and supporting details presented in diverse media and formats and explain how the ideas clarify a topic, text, or issue under study.

STARt thinking about what will happen in your favorite show.

TV Endings

Number of People: 2 Time: 5 minutes

Grade Level **7**

Materials: TV Programs

Description: Make TV watching valuable. At a commercial break, ask your child what's happened so far. What does he think will happen next? What other way might the story end? Language development and thinking skills can be built along with enjoying the entertaining aspects of the show.

ENGLISH LANGUAGE ARTS STANDARD

Speaking and Listening: Presentation of Knowledge and Ideas

4. Present claims and findings, emphasizing salient points in a focused, coherent manner with pertinent descriptions, facts, details, and examples; use appropriate eye contact, adequate volume, and clear pronunciation.

What we learned today...

Present It

Number of People: 2+ Time: Varies

Grade Level **7**

Materials: Reading material

Description: Talking often comes easily to a middle-schooler, so this time make the talking count. Ask your child to tell you about an event or topic and to use visuals to present the topic. My daughter learned Power-Point skills in 7th grade and uses them effectively. Ask about specific statements and why she chose certain points in her presentation. In case making a presentation isn't something she wants to do, reminder her that it's an effective way to talk about what she wants for Christmas or a birthday.

ENGLISH LANGUAGE ARTS STANDARD

Speaking and Listening: Presentation of Knowledge and Ideas

5. Include multimedia components and visual displays in presentations to clarify claims and findings and emphasize salient points.

What we learned today...

Trip Journal Two

Number of People: 2 Time: 15 minutes

Grade Level **7**

Materials: Paper or a notebook and pencil

Description: Suggest your teen keep a journal while on vacation. Where did you have breakfast? What time did you get to the restaurant? What did you eat? Was it good? What did it cost? Where did you travel for the day? What did you learn today? A lot happens on vacations. Have him write it down in his own words as soon as possible. Details are easy to forget and motivation wanes, so write soon.

ENGLISH LANGUAGE ARTS STANDARD

Language: Convention of Standard English

1. Demonstrate command of the conventions of standard English grammar and usage when writing or speaking.

Read To Me

Number of People: 2 Time: 20 minutes

Grade Level **7**

Materials: Writing assignments

Description: Have your teen read his writing assignments aloud. Reading to someone else helps discover errors in grammar, clarity, and completeness of thought. It can also help with punctuation, so encourage your child to read his written work with the periods and commas as he's written it. Check that pronouns match and verb tenses agree.

ENGLISH LANGUAGE ARTS STANDARD

Language: Conventions of Standard English

2. Demonstrate command of the conventions of standard English capitalization, punctuation, and spelling when writing.

Crosswords

Number of People: 2   Time: 30 minutes

Grade Level **7**

Materials: Crossword puzzle books

Description: When you read the newspaper, show your child the daily crossword. Let him do a crossword puzzle at his level of ability while you finish the paper or tackle the crossword yourself. There are crosswords for kids at your local newsstands, kids magazines, or looking up kids crosswords on the Internet. I will bet he does better on his crossword than you do on yours.

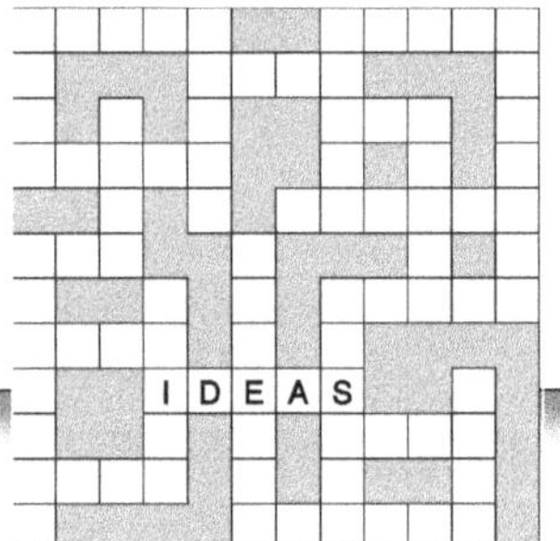

ENGLISH LANGUAGE ARTS STANDARD

Language Standard: Conventions of Standard English

2. Demonstrate command of the conventions of standard English capitalization punctuation and spelling when writing.

   B. Spell correctly.

Ologies

Number of People: 1+   Time: 30 minutes

Grade Level **7**

Materials: Dictionary, science book, or the Internet

Description: Biology is the study of life. "Bio" means life while "ology" means the science or study of. Let your child find as many "ologies" as he can. Physiology, meteorology, and neurology are just a few to start with, but there are many more. Have him figure out what each of the "ologies" that he finds is the study of a particular topic.

ENGLISH LANGUAGE ARTS STANDARD

Language Standard: Vocabulary Acquisition and Use

4. Determine or clarify the meaning of unknown ad multiple-meaning words and phrases based on grade 7 reading and content, choosing flexibility from a range of strategies.

   B. Use common, grade-appropriate Greek or Latin affixes and roots as clues to the meaning of a word.

Holiday letters are great places for you to STAR in any special events of the day.

Holiday Letter

Number of People: 2 Time: Varies

Grade Level **7**

Materials: Paper and pencil or computer

Description: Every Christmas season we send a letter to all our friends. Let your child be in charge of his part of the letter this year. What important events have happened in his life? How would he share this with others? You can send a letter more often than once a year—St. Patrick's Day, Valentine's, or whenever you or your child decide to give friends an update. You'll want him to check for misspellings before the letter goes out. A dictionary or spell checker will help. Let him do the changing to get it right.

ENGLISH LANGUAGE ARTS STANDARD

Language: Knowledge of Language

3. Use knowledge of language and its conventions when writing, speaking, reading, or listening.

What we learned today...

START going to the library and you'll find an amazing world of fiction and facts.

Read-a-Thon

Number of People: 1+ Time: 30 minutes

Grade Level **8**

Materials: Good books to read

Description: Getting an active eighth grader to read isn't hard if the book(s) are interesting. Each child will have his own special interests so to keep cost down, try the library. After an especially good book have a discussion with your reader about what kept the story going. How did the dialogue get him from one place to the next? What incidents were most exciting? What was the best part?

ENGLISH LANGUAGE ARTS STANDARD

Reading: Literature

3. Analyze how particular lines of dialogue or incidents in a story or drama propel the action, reveal aspects if a character or drive a decision.

What we learned today...

Book Reading and Travel

Number of People: 1 Time: Varies

Grade Level **8**

Materials: Magazines and books

Description: Rather than allowing your teen to text their friends, leave the phone home and ask her to bring a book. Fiction books in your car are great for your teen to leave for when she "has nothing to do". She can read while you shop for their dinner or pick up the dry cleaning. In between stops, ask her to tell you what's happening after each stop. Be sure to ask about the main character and where the action is taking place.

ENGLISH LANGUAGE ARTS STANDARD

Reading: Literature

2. Determine a theme or central idea of a text and analyze its development over the course of the text, including its relationship to the characters, setting, and plot; provide an objective summary of the text.

Compare Books

Number of People: 2 Time: 10 minutes

Grade Level 

Materials: Two books written about the same time

Description: *Little Women* and *Tom Sawyer*, written about the same time (1870 ish), are classics and yet very different in writing, characters, and story. We had our kids reading weekly so it wasn't hard to find a couple of books to compare. Read and discuss two books written about the same time. How does the way each of the books is written make the story better? Include both the meaning of the books and the style the author used.

ENGLISH LANGUAGE ARTS STANDARD

Reading: Literature

5. Compare and contrast the structure of two or more texts and analyze how the differing structure of each text contributes to its meaning and style.

Book and a Movie

Number of People: 2+ Time: Varies

Grade Level 8

Materials: *Reading Materials*

Description: Several of the *Harry Potter* books are movies. Both you and your child can pick one of the books to read and then rent the movie. See if you can find the parts that are really close to the book and which ones don't match at all. See who can locate the most matches and who can find the most discrepancies.

ENGLISH LANGUAGE ARTS STANDARD

Reading: Literature: Integration of Knowledge and Ideas

7. Analyze the extent to which a filmed or live production of a story or drama stays faithful to or departs from the text or script, evaluating the choices made by the director or actors.

Prove It

Number of People: 2 Time: 30 minutes

Grade Level 

Materials: Reference materials—magazines, books, Internet

Description: Play "Prove It." Kids often make wide generalizations—all dogs are mean, the Yankees always win the pennant, Tiger Woods is the best golfer ever. Great statements but can he prove what he says? The next time one of these statements comes up you call "Prove It". He gets to find documentation that backs up the claim. A magazine article or an Internet piece will prove his point as long as he can show the evidence. Just be prepared when you make a statement, and he says, "So prove it".

ENGLISH LANGUAGE ARTS STANDARD

Reading: Informational Text

1. Cite the textual evidence that most strongly supports an analysis of what the text says explicitly as well as inferences drawn from the text.

Words to the Wise

Number of People: 2 Time: Varies

Grade Level **8**

Materials: Paper and pencil or computer

Description: There are many new vocabulary words in eighth grade, and it's a good time to get used to them. High school will be full of new words and concepts so start now. New vocabulary is just another time to head for the library to pick out non-fiction books, magazines, or reference materials about sports, photography, cars, cooking, computers, or any other interest. Ask your reader to fill you in on the newest terms so you won't be caught not knowing about the newest and the latest.

ENGLISH LANGUAGE ARTS STANDARD

Reading: Informational Text: Craft and Structure

4. Determine the meaning of words and phrases as they are used in a text, including figurative, connotative, and technical meanings; analyze the impact of specific word choices on meaning and tone, including analogies or allusions to other texts.

What we learned today...

Fun notes can sometimes STARtle your friends and family.

Letter Writing

Number of People: 1+ Time: 20 minutes

Grade Level **8**

Materials: Paper and pencil or computer

Description: While you're writing to your friends, let your child write a note too. Sending letters to grandparents, cousins, or friends, means a letter in return to read and answer. Letter writing is great writing and reading reinforcement.

ENGLISH LANGUAGE ARTS STANDARD

Writing: Production and Distribution of Writing

4. Produce clear and coherent writing in which the development, organization and style are appropriate to task, purpose, and audience.

What we learned today...

Reference It

Number of People: 2+ Time: 40 minutes Grade Level **8**

Materials: Paper and pencil, reference materials, stopwatch

Description: On a piece of paper, create several columns with titles in the columns. Titles might be capital cities, stores, ballplayers, makes of cars, food, plants, etc. Have one player call out a letter and another player call out a number, e.g. k and 5. The letter you'll use is the fifth letter from the letter k, e.g. K then l, m, n, o, p—the fifth letter is p. All players then have 10 minutes to find and write down every word they can think of that starts with the letter p. Reference books and the internet are okay to use. When 10 minutes are up, the one with the most correct words wins. Words are disqualified if they can't be fund in a reference source.

ENGLISH LANGUAGE ARTS STANDARD

Writing: Research to Build and Present Knowledge

8. Gather relevant information from multiple print and digital sources, using search terms effectively, assess the credibility and accuracy of each source; and quote or paraphrase the data and conclusions of others while avoiding plagiarism and following a standard format for citation

TV Endings Plus

Number of People: 2 Time: 20 minutes Grade Level **8**

Materials: TV programs

Description: Most middle-schoolers watch some TV. Choose one of their favorite shows to watch with her. When the show is over, her job is to ask you questions about the show. Your job is to have listened well enough that she can't stump you. She will make them hard so watch closely. Then it's your turn to ask her questions.

ENGLISH LANGUAGE ARTS STANDARD

Speaking & Listening: Comprehension and Collaboration

1c. Pose questions that connect the ideas of several speakers and respond to others' questions and comments with relevant evidence, observations, and ideas.

Speech Day

Number of People: 2 Time: 20 minutes

Grade Level **8**

Materials: Tape recorder

Description: Have your child tape record himself giving a speech on a topic of his choice. Listen to the speech together after it is recorded. Talk about possible changes. Record the speech again with the changes you discussed. See how it sounds with the revisions.

ENGLISH LANGUAGE ARTS STANDARD

Speaking and Listening: Presentation of Knowledge and Ideas

4. Present claims and findings, emphasizing salient points in a focused, coherent manner with relevant evidence, sound valid reasoning, and well-chosen details; use appropriate eye contact, adequate volume, and clear pronunciation.

Speak for Yourself

Number of People: 2 Time: Varies

Grade Level 

Materials: Location in which a transaction takes place

Description: It's easy to fall into slang and clichés at any age especially if your friends all speak the same language. However, speeches in class or conversations with adults don't always lend themselves to the same slang. When you go into a store, bank, restaurant (not fast food), etc., let your child ask the questions for a purchase or a transaction. He will quickly discover that slang doesn't work when trying to order his favorite meal. Transactions also build confidence in handling himself in getting a job or business situations.

ENGLISH LANGUAGE ARTS STANDARD

Speaking & Listening: Presentation of Knowledge and Ideas

6. Adapt speech to a variety of contexts and tasks, demonstrating command of formal English when indicated or appropriate.

How about speaking or writing about the STARS—either movie or galaxy type will do.

Punctuate It

Number of People: 2 Time: 20 Minutes

Grade Level **8**

Materials: Paper and pencil or computer, magazine or book

Description: Pick a paragraph about a favorite topic from a book or magazine. Write or type the paragraph on a piece of paper leaving out punctuation. Have your child figure out what you removed. Your teen may have some difference of opinion about what's correct. She could be right. There may be several ways to punctuate correctly.

ENGLISH LANGUAGE ARTS STANDARD

Language: Conventions or Standard English

2. Demonstrate command of the convention of standard English capitalization, punctuation, and spelling when writing.

What we learned today...

I still enjoy a cliché like "STAR of the show."

Old Sayings

Number of People: 2 Time: 30+ minutes

Grade Level **8**

Materials: Paper and pencil

Description: Old sayings and clichés have meanings. For the next week, write down every old saying or cliché you can think of or run across. "Beggars can't be choosers" or "The light at the end of the tunnel" are old sayings. Once you have a good list, ask your child to tell you what she thinks each one means. Talk to her about the ones she doesn't know, then have her listen for sayings too.

ENGLISH LANGUAGE ARTS STANDARD

Language: Vocabulary Acquisition and Use

4. Determine or clarify the meaning of unknown and multiple-meaning words or phrases based on grade 8 reading and content, choosing flexibly from a range of strategies.

Your Own Definition

Number of People: 2 Time: 20+ minutes

Grade Level **8**

Materials: None, but you could write definitions down and make your own dictionary.

Description: Most kids don't enjoy looking up words in a dictionary. So, let them create definitions in their own words. Try nouns like lamppost, garage, and pillow or verbs like play, run, or crave. For example, your child might say, "A garage is a place you're supposed to keep a car, but it can also be storage for a lawn mower, holiday ornaments, garden tools, and all the left over stuff we don't know what to do with and won't fit in the house". You can define words too, and both of you can share your definitions.

ENGLISH LANGUAGE ARTS STANDARD

Language: Vocabulary Acquisition and Use

4. Determine or clarify the meaning of unknown and multiple-meaning words or phrases based on grade 8 reading and content, choosing flexibly from a range of strategies.

C. consult general and specialized reference materials, both print and digital, to find the pronunciation of a word or determine or clarify its precise meaning or its part of speech.

Bring it On

Number of People: 2 Time: Varies

Grade Level 

Materials: Paper and pencil or computer

Description: Middle-schoolers seem to challenge everything from the color of a banana to global warming. Instead of fighting, encourage a daily dose of arguments, and instead of a verbal discussion, have her put it in writing. Pick a topic with which you differ, and let her get her ideas, reasons, and evidence behind her thinking on paper. Based on her rationale, you'll also be better prepared to say yes or no to—going to the show Saturday night, staying with a friend, buying a new jacket, ...

ENGLISH LANGUAGE ARTS STANDARD

Writing: Text Types and Purposes

1. Write arguments to support claims with clear reasons and relevant evidence.

STARtup your new gadgets with a little help from Trinidad!

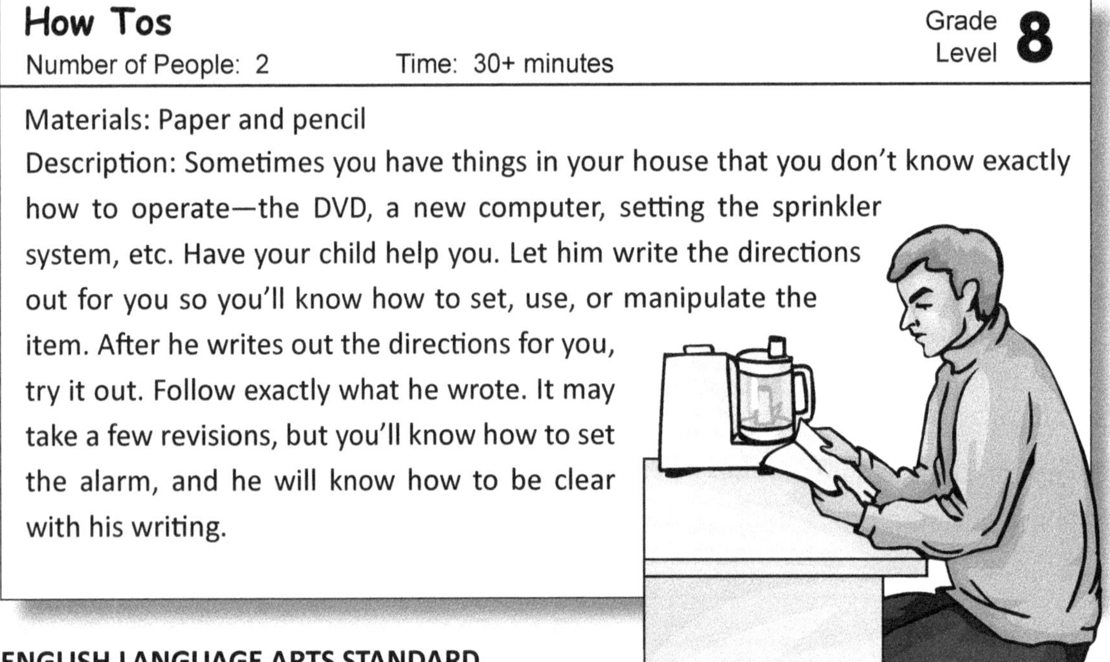

How Tos

Number of People: 2 Time: 30+ minutes

Grade Level **8**

Materials: Paper and pencil

Description: Sometimes you have things in your house that you don't know exactly how to operate—the DVD, a new computer, setting the sprinkler system, etc. Have your child help you. Let him write the directions out for you so you'll know how to set, use, or manipulate the item. After he writes out the directions for you, try it out. Follow exactly what he wrote. It may take a few revisions, but you'll know how to set the alarm, and he will know how to be clear with his writing.

ENGLISH LANGUAGE ARTS STANDARD

Writing: Text Types and Purposes

2. Write informative/explanatory texts to examine a topic and convey ideas, concepts, and information through the selection organization, and analysis of relevant content.

What we learned today...

Create your own playbook activities!

Language Arts Number of People: Time:	Grade Level
Materials: Description:	

ENGLISH LANGUAGE ARTS LEARNING STANDARD

Language Arts Number of People: Time:	Grade Level
Materials: Description:	

ENGLISH LANGUAGE ARTS LEARNING STANDARD

Create your own playbook activities!

Language Arts

Number of People: Time: Grade Level

Materials:

Description:

ENGLISH LANGUAGE ARTS LEARNING STANDARD

Language Arts

Number of People: Time: Grade Level

Materials:

Description:

ENGLISH LANGUAGE ARTS LEARNING STANDARD

MATH

6 - 8

Parent Playbook Activities

Want to add your favorite activity to the next Parent Playbook? Use the convenient form in the back of this book or contact the publisher at:

www.familyfriendlyschools.com • www.engagepress.com

By Dr. Joni Samples **Math Learning Standards**

MATH LEARNING STANDARDS
Grades 6-8

Mathematics Grade 6
- Ratios and Proportional Relationships
- The Number System
- Expressions and Equations
- Geometry
- Statistics and Probability

Mathematics Grade 7
- Ratios and Proportional Relationships
- The Number System
- Expressions and Equations
- Geometry
- Statistics and Probability

Mathematics Grade 8
- The Number System
- Expressions and Equations
- Functions
- Geometry
- Statistics and Probability

Little League

Number of People: 2 Time: 30 minutes

Grade Level 

Materials: Paper and pencil

Description: Let your child help you with Little League this year. If there are 16 teams with 14 players each, how many players are there in the league? If there is a $75 fee for each player, how much will the league have for the season? 19.12% of the money is spent on bats and balls. How much is that? Uniforms will cost 27.84% of the total. The umpires for each game will be 13.06% of the total and the grounds will require another 14%. How much will be left for the awards ceremony at the end? Change the numbers and the percentages, and there's lots more math to do.

Example: 16 X 14=224 players 224 X $75=$16,800

Bats and balls: $16,800 X 0.1912=$3212.16 Uniforms: $16,800X .2784=___

Umpires: $16,800 X .1306= ___

Grounds: ???? Awards: ????

MATH LEARNING STANDARD

Ratios & Proportional Relationships: Understand ratio concepts and use ratio reasoning to solve problems

3. Use ratio and rate reasoning to solve real-world and mathematical problems

Grocery Budget

Number of People: 2 Time: 30 minutes

Grade Level 

Materials: Grocery list, grocery section of the newspaper, paper and pencil

Description: Give your child your grocery list, a budget, and the grocery store advertisements from your local newspaper. Let him find your grocery list items in the advertisements. Ask him to calculate how much the total cost of your groceries for the week. Can he meet the budget? If not, what will he eliminate? If he stays under budget, how will your family spend the saved money?

MATH LEARNING STANDARD

Ratio & Proportional Relationships: Understand ratio concepts and use ratio reasoning to solve problems.

3b. solve unit rate problems including those involving unit pricing and constant speed.

Garage Sales

Number of People: 2 Time: Days

Grade Level 

Materials: Garage sale items, tags, paper and pencil

Description: Garage sales are fun. Have your child help organize one. He can clean out his room and other rooms in the house. Check to make sure he hasn't included your favorite pillow. Let him decide the price of each item. Once priced, let him calculate the total value if all items sold as he's priced them. What if they sold at 90% of their total value? How about 85% of their total value? What happens to his profits if items have to be cut in price? Let him prepare for the day of the sale, and let him handle the sales as they are made.

MATH LEARNING STANDARD

Ratios & Proportional Relationships: Understand ratio concepts and use ratio reasoning to solve problems

3c. Find a percent of a quantity as a rate per 100; solve problems involving finding the whole, given a part and the percent.

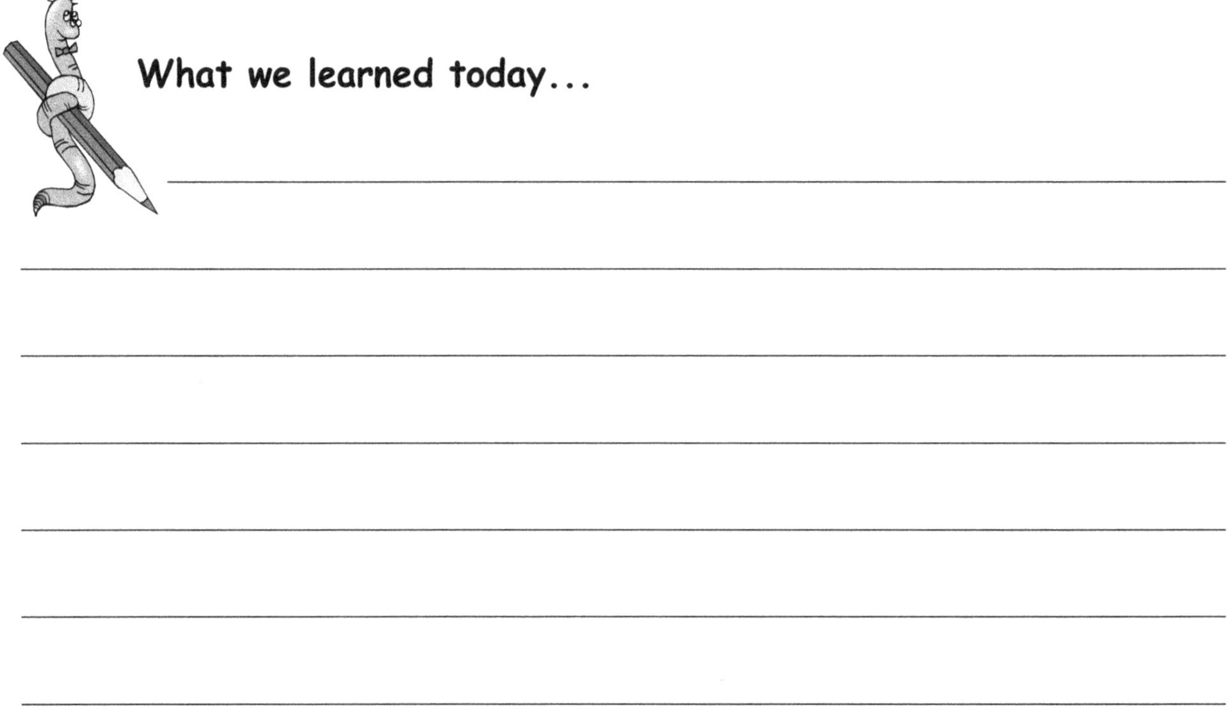

What we learned today...

Got Milk?

Number of People: 2 Time: Week

Grade Level **6**

Materials: Milk

Description: How many gallons of milk does your family drink during a week? How many ½ gallons? How many quarts? How many cups? How many pints? Does everyone drink the same amount? How much does each person drink?

MATH LEARNING STANDARD

Ratios & Proportional Relationships: Understand ratio concepts and use ratio reasoning to solve problems

3d. Use ratio reasoning to convert measurement units; manipulate and transform units appropriately when multiplying or dividing quantities.

Family Years

Number of People: 2 Time: 20 minutes

Grade Level **6**

Materials: Paper and pencil

Description: How old are the people in your family? Have your child estimate the total combined ages of the members of his family in years. Then have him estimate the combined age in months. Next, let him estimate the average age of your family members. Find out the actual age of each family member, complete the same calculations and compare the results.

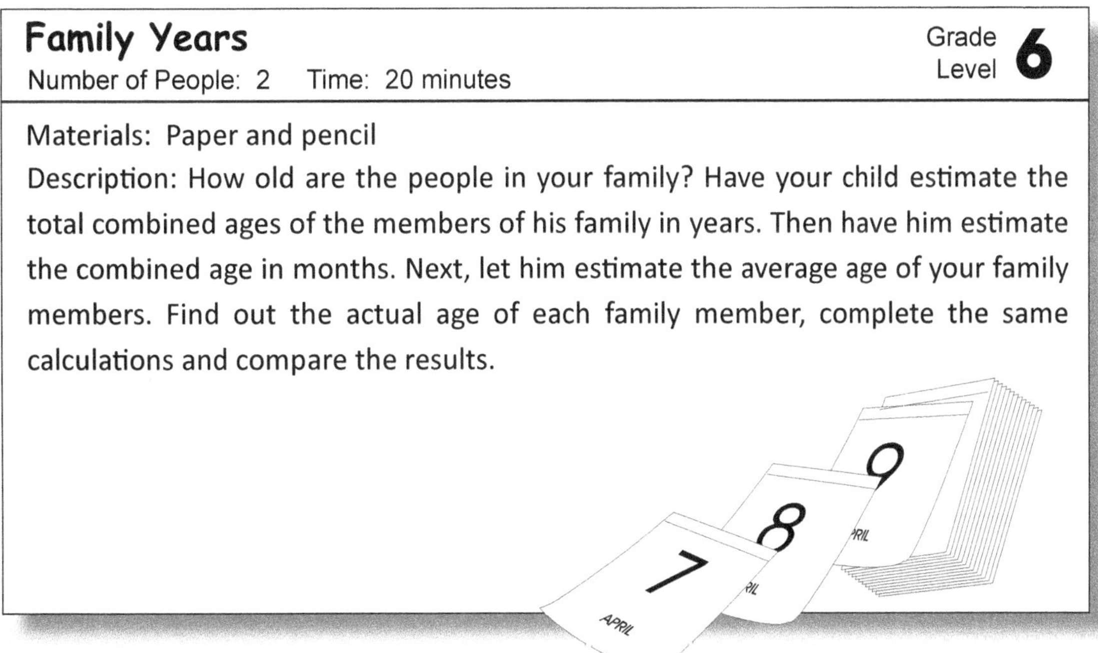

MATH LEARNING STANDARD

The Number System: Apply and extend previous understandings of multiplication and division divide fractions by fractions.

2. Fluently divide multi-digit numbers using the standard algorithm.

Stock Investments

Number of People: 2 Time: 30 minutes

Grade Level 

Materials: Paper and pencil, stock market pages

Description: Have your child invest money. (Use pretend money this time). Pretend she received $85 in birthday gifts. She invests it in stocks and in three years earns twelve percent per year. She takes the new amount and invests in a bond. She earns eight percent times as much on the new amount. After two years, she invests the new money in another stock which loses $50. How much money does she have? Change the amount of her start up capital and the investment percentages and see what happens.

Example:
Year 1: $85 X .12= $10.20 $85+$10.20=$95.20
Year 2: $95.20 X .12=11.42 $95.20+$11.42=$106.62
Year 3: 106.62 x .12=12.79 $106.62+$12.79=$119.41
Year 4: $119.42 X .08=9.55 $119.42+9.55= $128.97
Year 5: $128.97 X .08=10.32 $128.97+10.32= $139.29
Year 6: $139.29-$50=$89.29

MATH LEARNING STANDARD

The Number System

3. Fluently add, subtract, multiply, and divide multi-digit decimals using the standard algorithm for each operation.

Travel Miles

Number of People: 2 Time: Varies

Grade Level 

Materials: Paper and pencil, city map, car odometer

Description: If you have several errands to run, let your child calculate the number of miles you'll travel. What's the shortest route to take? How many miles between stops? How do you figure the mileage if you want the grocery store with the frozen foods to be your last stop?

MATH LEARNING STANDARD

The Number System:

3. Fluently add, subtract, multiply, and divide multi-digit decimals using the standard algorithm for each operation.

STARt out with a balanced money account and the world is yours.

Time to Pay Bills

Number of People: 2 Time: 20 minutes

Grade Level **6**

Materials: Paper and pencil

Description: When you pay bills, let your child help. Give her some multiplication and division problems using money while you work on your budget. You can start with Monopoly® money and move up to balance sheets. Kids often have trouble with dollars, decimals, and cents. Don't forget to compute interest.

MATH LEARNING STANDARD

The Number System:

3. Fluently add, subtract, multiply, and divide multi-digit decimals using the standard algorithm for each operation.

What we learned today...

Number Words

Number of People: 2 Time: 30 minutes Grade Level 

Materials: Paper and pencil

Description: Assign a single or double digit number to each letter of the alphabet. Some may have positive integers and some negative. For example: A= -93, B=+4, C=-76, etc. Have your child write ten words with ten letters each. Have your child match the letters with the numbers assigned to them. Then, have your child add the numbers together for each word. Which word has the highest score? What's the lowest? What's the score for all ten words? What's the score for the top five words? The lowest three? Try another set of words with eight letters in each word and see how many words she can come up with to reach a score between the total of 950 and 1,000.

Leadership= Additional=

MATH LEARNING STANDARD

The Number System: Apply and extend previous understandings of multiplication and division divide fractions by fractions.

5. Understand that positive and negative numbers are used together to describe quantities having opposite directions or values; use positive and negative numbers to represent quantities in real-world contexts, explaining the meaning of 0 in each situation.

What we learned today...

Family Ages

Number of People: 2 Time: 20 minutes

Grade Level 

Materials: Paper and pencil

Description: How old are the people in your family? Have your child graph the ages of the members of your family in years. On the vertical line of the graph put age ranges such as 0-10, 11-20, 21-30, etc. On the vertical line put the names/initials of family members. Adding grandchildren, cousins, and pets creates quite a conversation about why views may differ over what TV show to watch.

MATH LEARNING STANDARD

The Number System: Apply and extend previous understandings of numbers to the system of rational numbers

8. Solve real-world and mathematical problems by graphing points in all four quadrants of the coordinate plane.

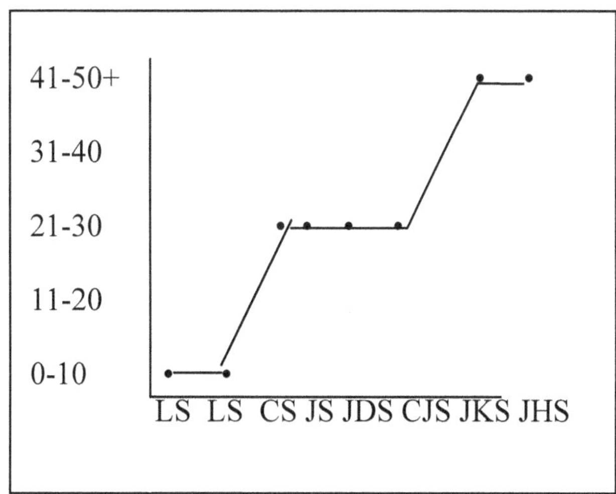

Simply Interested

Number of People: 2 Time: 20 minutes

Grade Level 

Materials: Paper and pencil

Description: Calculating the simple interest of a savings account is done by multiplying the principal by the rate of interest by the amount of time the interest will be paid (i=p x r x t). Let your child calculate the interest he would receive for $500 at 5% for a period of one year (500 x .05 x 1). Change the amount, the percentage, and the period of time. Just remember, the period of time is written as part of a year. For example, 6 months is ½ or.5 of a year. Help him open a savings account for practice.

Examples: interest=principal times rate times time

$500 X .05 X 1=$25

MATH LEARNING STANDARD

Expressions & Equations: Apply and extend previous understanding of arithmetic to algebraic expressions.

2. Write, read, and evaluate expression is which letters stand for numbers.

Math on Wheels

Number of People: 2+ Time: 20 minutes

Grade Level 

Materials: License plates

Description: While traveling, select a license plate. Using the digits on the plate, write down as many ways as you can to solve for a specific number. If the license number is TGY 4631, how many ways can you solve for 6? For example, (4+6) - (3+1) = 6. You get the picture. How many more can you find? Now change the solution to 8.

MATH LEARNING STANDARD

Expressions & Equations: Apply and extend previous understandings of arithmetic to algebraic expressions

3. Apply the properties of operations to generate equivalent expressions.

I especially like cornSTARCh and cuSTARd on my grocery list.

Change

Number of People: 2 Time: 10 minutes

Grade Level **6**

Materials: Groceries and money (pretend or real)

Description: If you estimate your groceries will be $37, ask your child to choose the bills he would give the clerk. If he gave the clerk two $20 bills, how much would he get back? If he gave the clerk a $50 bill, how much would he get back?

MATH LEARNING STANDARD

Expressions & Equations: Reason about and solve one-variable equations and inequalities

6. Use variable to represent numbers and write expressions when solving a real-world or mathematical problem; understand that a variable can represent an unknown number, or, depending on the purpose at hand, any number in a specified set.

What we learned today...

KickSTARt your allowance with a little extra work around the house or neighborhood.

Work Time

Number of People: 2   Time: Days

Grade Level 

Materials: Jobs to do, money, paper and pencil

Description: By middle school, most kids are looking to earn more money than their weekly allowance. At our house, we offer extra jobs the kids can do for extra pay. Washing windows, bringing in wood for the fireplace, or planting trees are just some of the extra tasks where they can help out. This is a great opportunity to teach your child how to create a budget. Have them put their budget in written form. How much will they save for the new bike they want? How much will they spend for CDs? How much for clothes? We use a budget to plan for our summer vacation.

MATH LEARNING STANDARD

Expression & Equations: Represent and analyze quantitative relationships between dependent and independent variables.

9. Use variable to represent two quantities in a real-world problem that change in relationship to one another; write an equation to express one quantity, thought of as the dependent variable, in terns of the other quantity, thought of an the independent variable.

What we learned today...

Yard Triangles

Number of People: 2 Time: 45 minutes

Grade Level 

Materials: Yard, stakes, string, measuring tape, paper and pencil

Description: One Saturday, have you and your child divide a portion of your yard into triangles with posts and string. Spend the morning figuring out the area of each of the triangles you've created. How would you do that? You can move the strings and measure until you get it or you can use a formula. There are several formulae for different shapes of triangles on the Internet or in your child's math book. Try several ways until it becomes easy.

MATH LEARNING STANDARD

Geometry: Solve real-world and mathematical problems involving area, surface area, and volume

1. Find the area of right triangles, other triangles, special quadrilaterals, and polygons by composing into rectangles or decomposing into triangles and other shapes; apply these techniques in the context of solving real-world mathematical problems

Bus Miles

Number of People: 2 Time: 20 minutes

Grade Level 6

Materials: A friendly bus driver, paper and pencil

Description: Riding a bus to school every day brings about some interesting questions. How many miles does your child's bus travel every day? Have your child ask all the students on the bus how far they think the bus travels. Have her average the answers. Let her check with the bus driver for the exact mileage. On a different bus, have her ask only ten of the students how far they think the bus travels daily. Again, ask the bus driver for the exact mileage. Which survey was closer, the total population or the sample? Which was easier to do? When will she use each kind of survey?

MATH LEARNING STANDARD

Statistics & Probability: Develop understanding of statistical variability

1. Recognize a statistical question as one that anticipates variability in the data related to the question and accounts for it in the answers.

Weigh It

Number of People: 2 Time: 10 minutes

Grade Level 

Materials: Bag of groceries, bag of potatoes, scale

Description: How much does your bag of potatoes weigh? Let your child fill and weigh several bags of potatoes. What is the average (mean) of the sacks she's weighed? The average can be found by adding the weights of all the bags together and dividing by the total number of bags. What is the difference (range) between the weight of the lightest bag of potatoes and the heaviest bag of potatoes? What is the weight of the bag in the middle (median) of the lightest bag and the heaviest bag? Which bag is the best for your family?

MATH LEARNING STANDARD

Statistics & Probability: Summarize and describe distributions

5c. Giving quantitative measures of center (median and/or mode) and variability (interquartile range and/or mean absolute deviation), as well as describing any overall pattern and any striking deviations from the overall pattern with reference to the context in which the data were gathered.

Let's Go To the Show

Number of People: 2 Time: 30 minutes

Grade Level 

Materials: Paper and pencil, movie ads

Description: Going to the movies is fun and many people go. If 465 people go to your favorite movie theater on a Saturday night, and there are four different movies playing, let your child figure out how many people went to each movie. Movie number one sold 2/5 of the total ticket sales. The second movie sold 30% of the total tickets sold. Of the remaining sales 60% went to the third movie and the rest went to the fourth movie. How many people went to each? Change the numbers, the fractions, and the percentages and you have plenty of calculations to do. Add in the price of tickets and see how much money is involved.

MATH LEARNING STANDARD

Ratios and Proportional Relationships

1. Compute unit rates associated with ratios of fractions, including ratios of lengths, areas and other quantities measured in like or different units.

I'm pretty partial to the Lone STAR state myself.

Square Miles

Number of People: 2 Time: 30 minutes

Grade Level **7**

Materials: Map of the U.S., information on size of states (Internet or encyclopedia), paper and pencil

Description: In this exercise, you can combine a little math and a little geography. Have your child pick ten states and then look up each state's size in square miles. Ask him to rank the states in order of square miles from the largest state to the smallest state. What's the total number of square miles in all ten states? What percentage of the total is the third state on your list? What percentage of the total is your state? What's the difference between the largest and the smallest state? You might discover some new places you'd like to visit while doing this activity.

MATH LEARNING STANDARD

Ratios & Propositional Relationships: Analyze proportional relationships and use them to solve real-world and mathematical problems

2b. Identify the constant of proportionality in tables, graphs, equations, diagrams, and verbal descriptions of proportional relationships.

What we learned today...

Movie Fun

Number of People: 2+ Time: 20 Minutes

Grade Level **7**

Materials: Paper and pencil

Description: Going to the movies can be fun, but it can also be expensive. If a movie cost $3.25 for adults and $2.75 for children your child can figure out how much it would cost to take your family, your family and four friends, or your family and half the neighborhood. Have your child put the calculation into an equation so it will be easy to figure out each time you go to the movies no matter how many go with you.

MATH LEARNING STANDARD

Ratios and Proportional Relationships: Analyze proportional relationships and use them to solve real-world and mathematical problems.

What we learned today...

Time To Go - II

Number of People: 2 Time: Varies

Grade Level **7**

Materials: Car

Description: While running errands, let your child figure out if you're going to be late. It's 3:15 pm and you have to be at the dentist by 4:00 pm. It takes 35 minutes to get across town. Will you make it? It's 5:30 pm and you're driving thirty miles an hour. Soccer practice begins at 6:20 pm. When will you arrive at the soccer field? You can create many of these time mileage activities.

MATH LEARNING STANDARD

Ratios & Proportional Relationships: Analyze proportional relationships and use them to solve real-world and mathematical problems

3. Use proportional relationships to solve multistep ratio and percent problems.

Cataloging Your Budget

Number of People: 2 Time: 30 minutes

Grade Level **7**

Materials: Catalogs, paper and pencil

Description: Have your child go through a catalog and choose items he would like to purchase. Give him a budget, and let him add up his choices to see if he can stay within his budget. He may have to make some changes. Remind him this is pretend–at least until his birthday.

MATH LEARNING STANDARD

The Number System: Apply and extend previous understandings of operations with fractions to add, subtract, multiply, and divide rational numbers.

1. Apply and extend previous understandings of addition and subtraction to add and subtract rational numbers; represent addition and subtraction on a horizontal or vertical number line diagram.

Age Old Hours

Number of People: 2 Time: 30 minutes

Grade Level **7**

Materials: Paper and pencil

Description: Dan is 187,324 hours old. How old does your child think Dan is? Let her estimate her own age in hours. How old is she? Let her calculate Dan's age in months and then in years. Let her do the same with her own age. Tim is 432,917 hours old. How old does she think he is? How old is he? You can ask any number of these questions. Estimation is an important skill and doing the calculations is great math practice.

MATH LEARNING STANDARD

The Number System: Apply and extend previous understandings of operations with fractions to add, subtracts, multiply, and divide rational numbers.

1. Apply and extend previous understandings of addition and subtraction to add and subtract rational numbers; represent addition and subtraction on a horizontal or vertical number line diagram.

Time Comparisons

Number of People: 2 Time: Varies

Grade Level **7**

Materials: Watch with a second hand or stop watch

Description: Let your child time a commercial. Have her time a TV show. Next have her time how long it takes to clean a room. Kids think it takes four hours to clean a room and five minutes for a TV show. Let her graph the time so she can see the difference, and hopefully stop arguing with you.

MATH LEARNING STANDARD

The Number System: Apply and extend previous understandings of operations with fractions to add, subtract, multiply, and divide rational numbers.

1d. Apply properties of operations as strategies to add and subtract rational numbers.

Being able to do math makes you a SuperSTAR!

Million or Double Your Money?

Number of People: 2 Time: 30 minutes

Grade Level **7**

Materials: Paper and pencil, calculator

Description: Ask your child which he would prefer: $1,000,000 or a month's worth of doubling one dollar. Start with a dollar on the first day of the month. On the second day double the amount of the first day. Therefore, on day two he will have two dollars. On day three double day two. Now he has four dollars. He will have sixteen dollars on day four. Keep going for thirty days. Let him calculate the month's doubling before he makes his choice.

MATH LEARNING STANDARD

The Number System: Apply and extend previous understanding of operations with fractions to add, subtract, multiply, and divide rational numbers.

2. Apply and extend previous understandings of multiplication and division and of fractions to, multiply and divide rational numbers

What we learned today...

How long have your favorite COSTARs been in the TV series you like best?

Best of Times

Number of People: 2   Time: 30 minutes

Grade Level **7**

Materials: Paper and pencil

Description: Ask your child to give you a period of time in a different form. For example, "Tim, you're twelve years old. How many days old are you? How many minutes until your next birthday? How many seconds until your alarm clock goes off? Tennis practice is three hours long. How many minutes is that? Your favorite TV show has been running for five seasons. With thirty-two shows in a season and each show is forty-seven minutes, how many minutes has the show run? How many days? Try your own combinations.

MATH LEARNING STANDARD

Expressions & Equations: Use properties of operations to generate equivalent expressions.

1. Apply properties of operations as strategies to add, subtract, factor, and expand linear expressions with rational coefficients

What we learned today...

Sales Tax

Number of People: 2 Time: 15 minutes

Grade Level **7**

Materials: Newspaper ads

Description: Shopping is always fun, but don't let your child forget to add in the sales tax when calculating your check out price. If he's buying a CD for $14.99 with a 7.25% sales tax, what will the cost of the CD be? Use an advertisement from the newspaper and let him choose five items with different prices. Add in the sales tax. What will his total be? What would it be with a different sales tax amount?

MATH LEARNING STANDARD

Expressions & Equations: Solve real-life and mathematical problems using numerical and algebraic expressions and equations

3. Solve multi-step real-life and mathematical problems posed with positive and negative rational numbers in any form, using tool strategically.

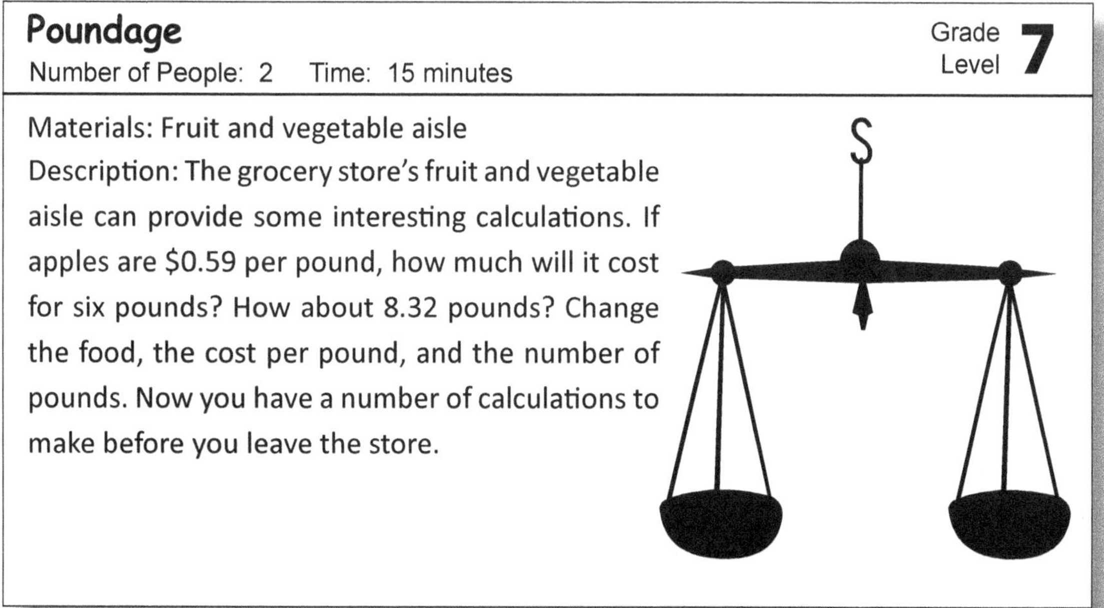

Poundage

Number of People: 2 Time: 15 minutes

Grade Level **7**

Materials: Fruit and vegetable aisle

Description: The grocery store's fruit and vegetable aisle can provide some interesting calculations. If apples are $0.59 per pound, how much will it cost for six pounds? How about 8.32 pounds? Change the food, the cost per pound, and the number of pounds. Now you have a number of calculations to make before you leave the store.

MATH LEARNING STANDARD

Expressions & Equations: Solve real-life and mathematical problems using numerical and algebraic expressions and equations

3. solve multi-step real-life and mathematical problems posed with positive and negative rational numbers in any form, using tools strategically.

Compound Your Interest

Number of People: 2 Time: 30+ minutes

Grade Level **7**

Materials: Paper and pencil, bank interest rates

Description: Simple interest is calculated by multiplying principal by rate of interest by time (i = p x r x t). If your child started with $500 and received 5% interest for one year, the interest would be $25 ($500 x .05 x 1 = $25). If the interest were compounded quarterly, the amount gained would change every three months or ¼ of the year. After the first quarter, the interest would be calculated and added to the principal ($500 x .05 x .25 = $6.25; $6.25 + $500 = $506.25). The second quarter would start with a principal of $506.25. Continue to calculate the next three quarters with the additional amount added to each quarter. This will net quite an increase over the simple interest. Have your child calculate the amount. Change the principal and see what happens.

MATH LEARNING STANDARD

Expressions & Equations: Solve real-life and mathematical problems using numerical and algebraic expressions and equations.

4. Use variables to represent quantities in a real-world or mathematical problem, and construct simple equations and inequalities to solve problems by reasoning about the quantities.

Rearrange Time

Number of People: 2 Time: 20 Minutes

Grade Level **7**

Materials: paper (graph paper is best), pencil, ruler

Description: It's time to rearrange the furniture in your child's room and he can do it. First, though, you'll need a drawing to know how to do it. Have your child draw his room to scale. Include furniture to scale so you can move it around to get it just right. You might want a different scale to take to the store to find the right paint. Let him do that one too.

MATH LEARNING STANDARD

Geometry: Draw construct, and describe geometrical figures and describe the relationships between them.

1. Solve problems involving scale drawings of geometric figures, including computing actual lengths and areas from a scaled drawing and reproducing a scale drawing at a different scale.

Pizza Size

Number of People: 2 Time: 15 minutes Grade Level **7**

Materials: Pizza menu, paper and pencil

Description: When we want pizza at my house, we need a large one. How large do you want your pizza? Have your child measure the radius which is half the distance across the pizza. To find the area of the pizza use the formula Area = πr^2. Pi (π) equals 3.1416. Have him calculate the area of the Pizza Factory pizza. Is it bigger than the one from Pizza Hut? How big is their biggest pizza? How big is the smallest? Which size do you need for your family?

MATH LEARNING STANDARD

Geometry: solve real-life and mathematical problems involving angle measure, area, surface area, and volume

4. Know the formulas for the area and circumference of a circle and use them to solve problems; give an informal derivation of the relationship between the circumference and area of a circle.

What we learned today...

Sale Prices

Number of People: 2+ Time: 30 minutes

Grade Level **7**

Materials: Grocery items

Description: Once a week I find myself at the grocery store with one or more of my kids. They help. One child checks prices and sales. Is the 22 oz. jar for $1.98 a better deal than the 44 oz. jar for $4.05? Another keeps a running amount of how much we've spent so we don't go over budget. Another child is in charge of the coupons. She finds the coupon items and keeps track of what is left on our list. It takes a lot to feed a family of six. They stay busy. Encourage your child to become a part of your family's grocery store experience. Occasionally we can slip in something a bit more complicated like $\$2.50^2=6.25$. Scientific notation in the grocery store. Imagine that!

NATIONAL MATH STANDARD

Expressions and Equations:

4. Perform operations with numbers expressed in scientific notation, including problems where both decimal and scientific notation are used.

Win the Lottery

Number of People: 2 Time: 30 Minutes

Grade Level **7**

Materials: Paper and pencil, a list of relatives

Description: If a long lost relative passed away and left your family an inheritance, how would it be divided? Let your preteen do the calculations. If the inheritance was for $9,742 and there are twelve members in the family, how much did each receive? If each family member gave his or her money to four charities how much did each charity receive? Change the amounts and try again.

NATIONAL MATH STANDARD

Statistics & Probability: Investigate chance processes and develop use, and evaluate probability models

5. Understand that the probability of a chance event is a number between 0 and 1 that expresses the likelihood of the event occurring. Larger numbers indicate greater likelihood. A probability near 0 indicates an unlikely event, a probability around 1/2 indicates an event that is nether unlikely nor likely, and a probability near 1 indicates a likely event.

STARtling sometimes how much time we spend in certain activities. My favorite is a day at the beach.

Chart It

Number of People: 2 Time: 24 Hours Grade Level 

Materials: Chart paper and pencil, colored pencils

Description: Have your teen keep track of how he spends his time in a 24-hour period. Have him chart his time sleeping, eating, playing, and learning on a bar chart. Now use a pie chart and compare. Is he surprised at the amount of time he sleeps in comparison to the time he plays? Include the time for doing chores. My children always think they do hours of chores and are surprised when they find chores take only a fraction of the time.

NATIONAL MATH STANDARDS

Statistics & Probability: Investigate chance processes and develop, use, and evaluate probability models.

7. Develop a probability model and use it to find probabilities of events. Compare probabilities from a model to observed frequencies; if the agreement is not good, explain possible sources of the discrepancy.

How Much Time?

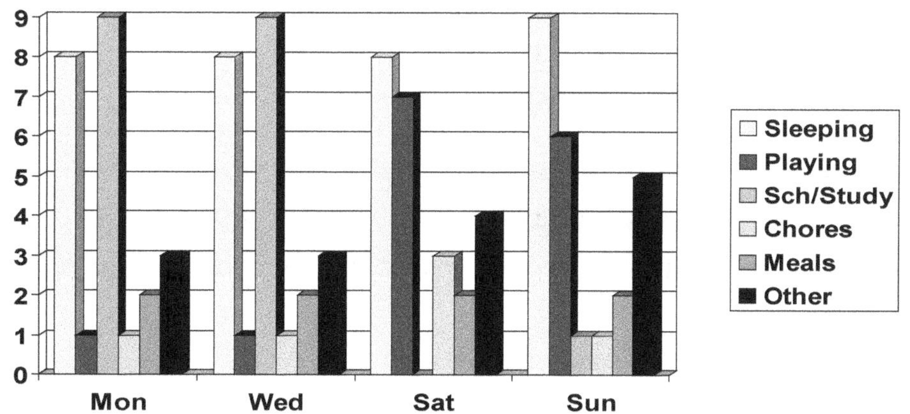

Exponentially Simple

Number of People: 2 Time: 20 minutes

Grade Level **8**

Materials: Paper and pencil, math book

Description: Sometimes math just needs problems to solve that you don't use around the house much. One might be exponents. I would love to use exponents in my checkbook. $10 to the ^{2} or ^{3}. Have your child try that on their allowance. How much would it be to the third power? How long would it take to earn that much?

NATIONAL MATH STANDARD

Expression & Equations: Expressions and Equations work with radical and integer exponents

1. Know and apply the properties of integer exponents to generate equivalent numerical expressions.

Travel Time

Number of People: 2 Time: 30 minutes

Grade Level **8**

Materials: Paper and pencil

Description: Ask your child how long it will take to get to your destination if you are traveling thirty miles and the speed limit is sixty miles per hour. Once she figures out the formula, make the calculation more difficult by changing the travel length to forty nine miles. Try it again with seventy-two miles. Change the speed limit to fifty miles and seventy miles per hour.

NATIONAL MATH STANDARD

Expression & Equations: Analyze and solve linear equations and pairs of simultaneous linear equations

7. Solve linear equations in one variable.

Birth Formula

Number of People: 2 Time: 30 minutes

Grade Level 

Materials: Paper and pencil

Description: Here's a fun formula using the month of your child's birth. Begin with the number of his birth month. Add 32 to the number or B + 32 = __. Then, add the difference of his birth month and twelve or B + 32 + (12 – B) = __. Next, divide by 2 or B+32+(12-B) divided by 2= then add 6

The answer is 28. It's always 28. Try it.

NATIONAL MATH STANDARD

Expression & Equations: Analyze and solve linear equations and pairs of simultaneous linear equations.

7. Solve linear equations in one variable.

What we learned today...

Graph Your Location

Number of People: 2 Time: 20 minutes

Grade Level **8**

Materials: Map with longitude and latitude lines

Description: Graphing equations can be difficult to grasp at first. One way to see how points on a graph work is to look at longitude and latitude lines on a map. The equator is the X axis and Greenwich is the Y axis. Have your child find your location on the plane. Using your map coordinates, where are his grandparents on the plane?

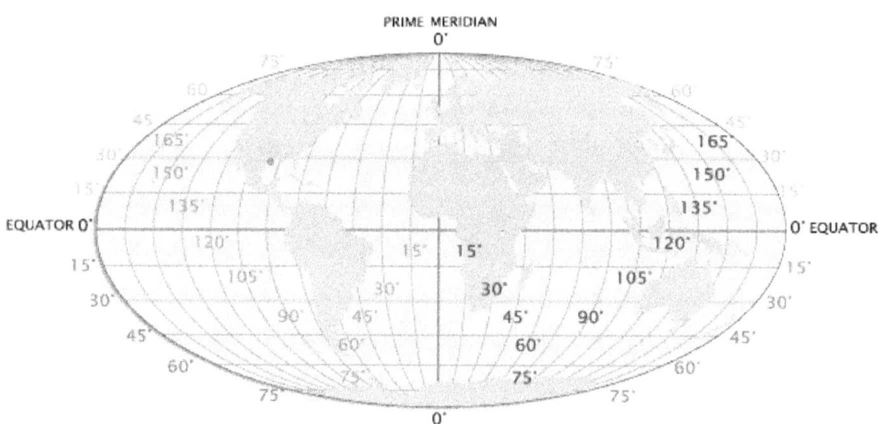

NATIONAL MATH STANDARD

Function: Use functions to model relationships between quantities.

4. Describe qualitatively the functional relationship between two quantities by analyzing a graph. Sketch a graph that exhibits the qualitative features of a function that has been descried verbally.

Another Triangular Day

Number of People: 2+ Time: 15 mins

Grade Level **8**

Materials: Posts, string, measuring tape, paper, pencil

Description: Last year you and your child turned your yard into triangles. This year do it again. Only this time make it all right triangles. Lay them out with posts and string. Measure two sides and use the Pythagorean Theorem ($a^2 + b^2 = c^2$) to figure the third. Try it on each of your triangles. Bet this is one formula your child won't forget.

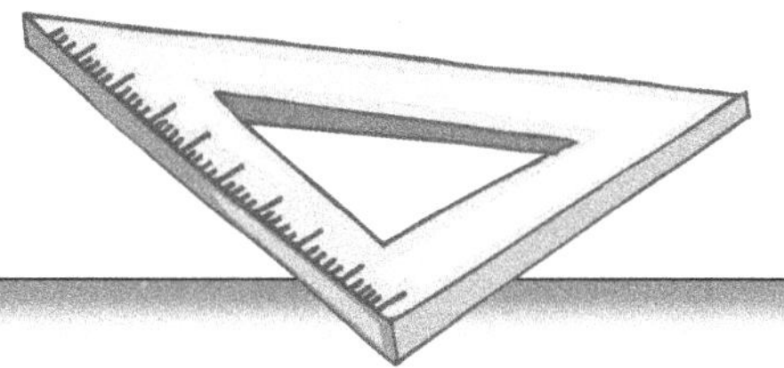

NATIONAL MATH STANDARD

Geometry: Understand and apply the Pythagorean Theorem

7. Apply the Pythagorean Theorem to determine unknown side lengths in right triangles in real-world and mathematical problems in two and three dimensions.

Women's Salaries

Number of People: 2 Time: 45 minutes

Grade Level 

Materials: Paper and pencil, graph on next page

Description: A newspaper story reported women's salaries are catching up to men's salaries. Have your teen use the information on the following page to design a line graph to see if the gap is growing or closing. She can also check to see the percentage of increase by subtracting the lowest men's salary from the highest men's salary and then divide the difference by the lowest men's salary. Do the same for the women's salaries. Will the lines on the graph ever cross?

NATIONAL MATH STANDARD

Statistics & Probability: Investigate patterns of association in bivariate data

1. Construct and interpret scatter plots for bivariare measurement data to investigate patterns of association between two quantities.

Year	Median Women's Salary	Median Men's Salary	Salary Difference
1996	$14,682	$27,248	$12,566
1997	$15,573	$28,919	$13,346
1998	$17,716	$28,755	
1999	$18,440	$30,079	
2000	$20,267	$30,951	
2001	$20,851	$31,364	
2002	$21,429	$31,647	
2003	$22,004	$32,048	
2004	$22,256	$32,483	
2005	$23,074	$34,349	
2006	$24,466	$35,879	
2007	$25,878	$36,635	

What we learned today...

Create your own playbook activities!

Math
Number of People: Time: Grade Level

Materials:

Description:

MATH LEARNING STANDARD

Math
Number of People: Time: Grade Level

Materials:

Description:

MATH LEARNING STANDARD

Create your own playbook activities!

Math		Grade Level
Number of People:	Time:	

Materials:

Description:

MATH LEARNING STANDARD

Math		Grade Level
Number of People:	Time:	

Materials:

Description:

MATH LEARNING STANDARD

SCIENCE

6 – 8

Parent Playbook Activities

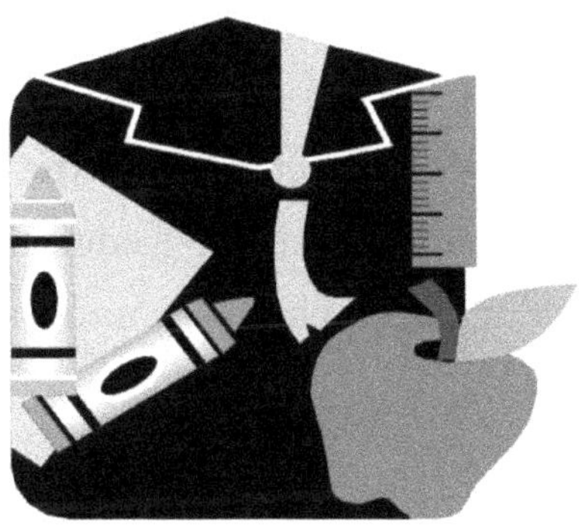

Want to add your favorite activity to the next Parent Playbook? Use the convenient form in the back of this book or contact the publisher at:

www.familyfriendlyschools.com • www.engagepress.com

By Dr. Joni Samples **Science Learning Standards**

SCIENCE LEARNING STANDARDS
Grades 6-8

The purpose of Learning Standards is to enable all students to achieve scientific literacy. The standards used for the activities on the following pages are a compilation of standards used in districts across the nation.

The K-8 standards are a continuous roadmap of knowledge building one skill upon another. This roadmap tells us how to get to the final destination. Scientific literacy is of increasing importance in our workplace. More and more jobs demand advanced science skills.

The Science Learning Standards provide expectations for the development of student understanding and ability over the course of their K-8 education. We have listed the Science Learning Standards on the following page to help you understand how each activity connects to each standard.

Standard A: Science as Inquiry

- Abilities necessary to do scientific inquiry
- Understanding about scientific inquiry

Standard B: Physical Science

- Properties of objects and materials
- Position and motion of objects
- Light, heat, electricity, and magnetism

Standard C: Life Science

- Characteristics of organisms
- Life cycles of organisms
- Organisms and environment

Standard D: Earth and Space Science

- Properties of earth materials
- Objects in the sky
- Changes in earth and sky

Standard E: Science and Technology

- Abilities of technological design
- Understandings about science and technology
- Abilities to distinguish between natural objects and objects made by humans

Standard F: Science in Personal and Social Perspectives

- Personal Health
- Characteristics and changes in population
- Types of resources
- Change in the environments
- Science and technology in local challenges

Standard G: History and Nature of Science

- Science as a human endeavor
- Nature of science
- History of science

Measure It

Number of People: 2 Time: Varies

Grade Level 

Materials: Metric measuring device, area to measure

Description: Have your child measure her room. You may have done this when she was younger, but now have her measure using the metric system. Have her use the data she's obtained to draw a scaled picture of her room. She can make changes to the location of furniture and other items. What is the best use of her space?

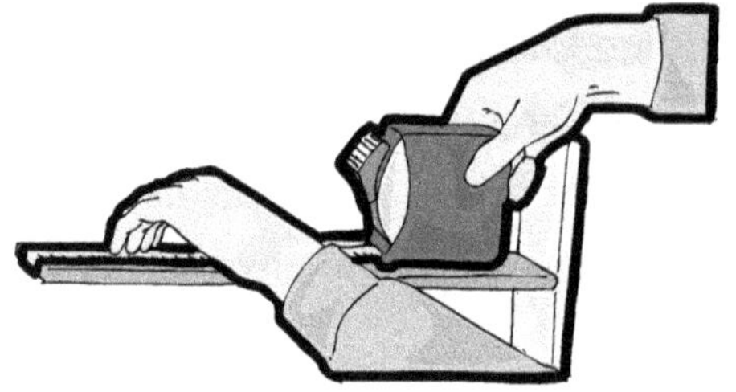

SCIENCE LEARNING STANDARD A 1

Essential Skill Activity:

The use of tools and techniques including math will be guided by questions asked and student designs.

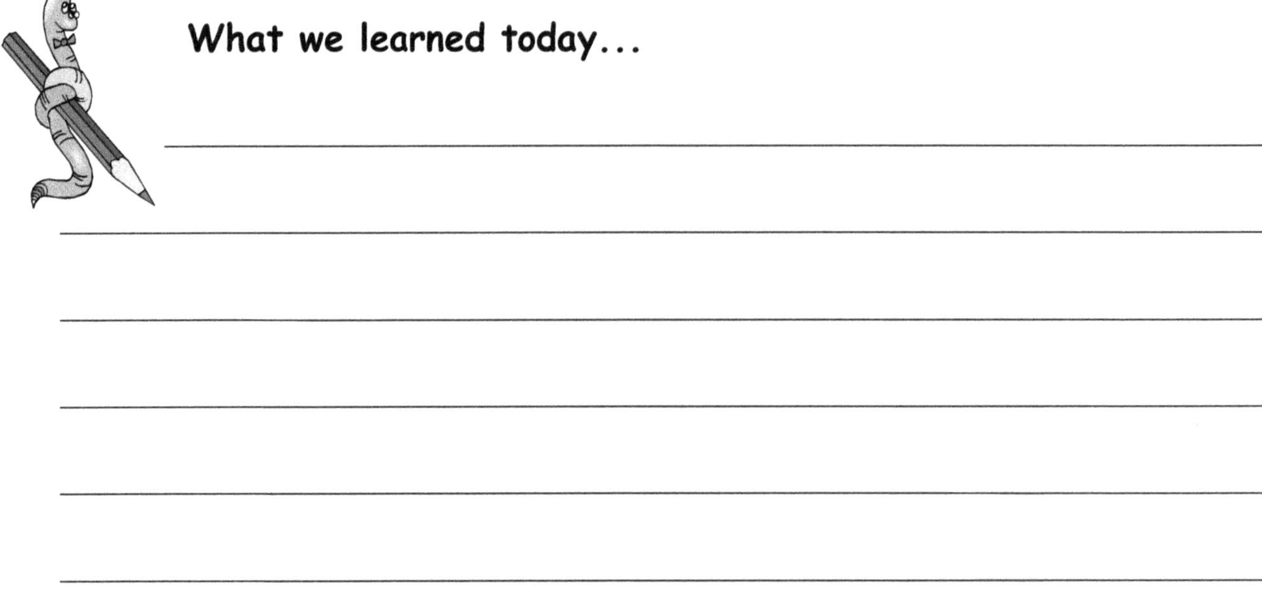

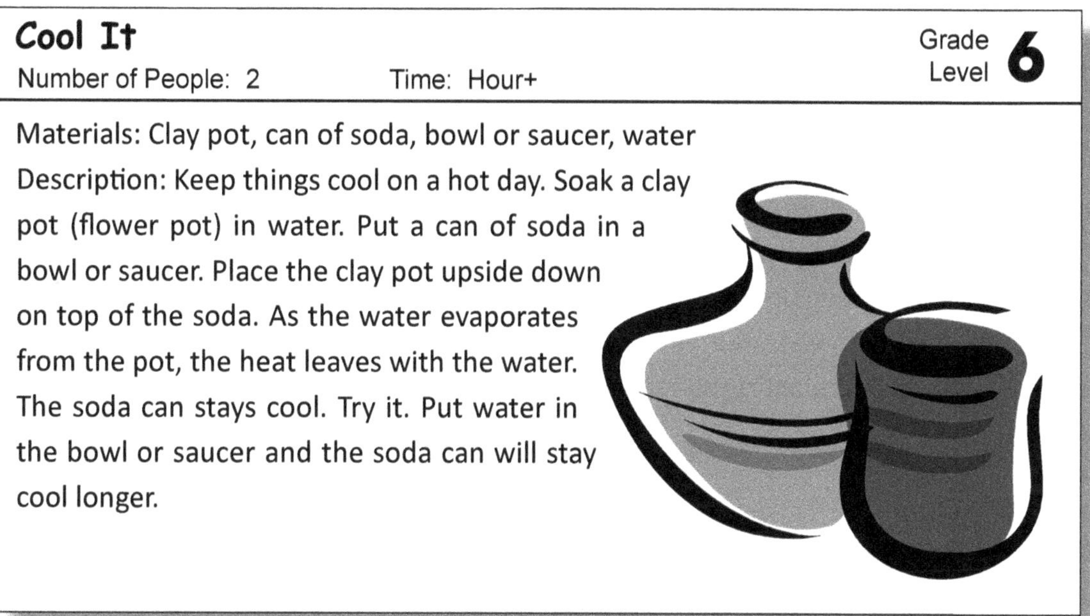

Cool It

Number of People: 2 Time: Hour+ Grade Level 6

Materials: Clay pot, can of soda, bowl or saucer, water

Description: Keep things cool on a hot day. Soak a clay pot (flower pot) in water. Put a can of soda in a bowl or saucer. Place the clay pot upside down on top of the soda. As the water evaporates from the pot, the heat leaves with the water. The soda can stays cool. Try it. Put water in the bowl or saucer and the soda can will stay cool longer.

SCIENCE LEARNING STANDARDS D 3 & A 1

Essential Skill Activity:

Kids learn that the sun is the major source of energy for phenomenon both on the earth's surface and of tides.

Kids learn to create questions that can be answered through scientific investigations.

Electric Balloons

Number of People: 2 Time: 10 minutes Grade Level 

Materials: 2 balloons, string, plastic wrap

Description: Learn about electrical charges. All you need is two balloons and a piece of plastic wrap. Inflate the balloons and tie a string on each end. Have your child rub each balloon with a piece of plastic wrap. Have him hold the ends of the strings. Allow the sides of the balloon to touch. What happens? Now rub one balloon with plastic wrap and hold the plastic wrap two inches from the balloon. What happens? He's created an electrical charge. Like charges repel each other while opposite charges attract each other. What type of charge has he created? See what else will attract or repel your balloons.

SCIENCE LEARNING STANDARD B 3

Essential Skill Activity:

Energy is a property of many substances and is associated with heat, light, electricity, mechanical motion, sound and the nature of chemicals.

Weatherman

Number of People: 2 Time: 30 minutes

Grade Level 

Materials: Newspaper, Internet, or TV nightly news with weather reports

Description: Have your child check the weather report in the newspaper, on the Internet, or by watching the nightly weather report on your local TV station. Have him keep a weather chart so he can keep up with weather trends. Many discussions can be generated about seasons, clothes to wear, and when to plant rutabagas.

SCIENCE LEARNING STANDARD D 1

Essential Skill Activity:

Water circulates through the crust, oceans, and atmosphere in what is known as the "water cycle".

Sand Castles Are For Big Kids Too

Number of People: 2+ Time: Varies

Grade Level 

Materials: Sand, water

Description: Making sand castles on the beach offers your child an opportunity to learn architecture and design skills. She will need to develop the right mixture of sand and water and make choices about adding walls and bridges Questions about how sand became part of the beach, or what part water plays in the process of moving sand, or how sand is affected by river and ocean movement, may not help with building a better sand castle, but they will tell you where to find the next beach.

SCIENCE LEARNING STANDARDS D 2 & D 3

Essential Skill Activity:

Students learn that beaches are dynamic systems in which the sand is supplied by rivers and moved along the coast by the action of waves.

Science includes weather, plants, animals, and so much more. I particularly like STARgazing.

Drying the Wash

Number of People: 2 Time: Hour+

Grade Level **6**

Materials: Sheet, scissors, clothes washer

Description: What are the best drying conditions for your laundry? Cut an old sheet into five pieces. Put the pieces in the washing machine. When they are finished, it's time to see which conditions are best for drying. Have your child hang one piece of cloth in a breeze and one where the air is still. Lay one piece in the shade and another in the sun. Wad one piece into a ball. Which one dries first? Why? What makes the difference?

SCIENCE LEARNING STANDARD D 3

Essential Skill Activity:

Kids learn that the sun is the major source of energy for phenomenon both on earth's surface and of tides. It powers winds, ocean currents and the water cycle.

What we learned today...

You can protect your water as well as the water for us STARfish. We find it pretty important stuff.

Water Quality

Number of People: 2 Time: Hour

Grade Level **6**

Materials: Internet, paper and pencil

Description: Your child may not realize the water in our streams and lakes is monitored regularly, often by volunteers. Check out your local U.S. Environmental Protection Agency or go online and get information from their website. You can find out how to protect the water you drink. Have your child make a list of things you need to do to have renewable, safe drinking water. You may even decide to volunteer together.

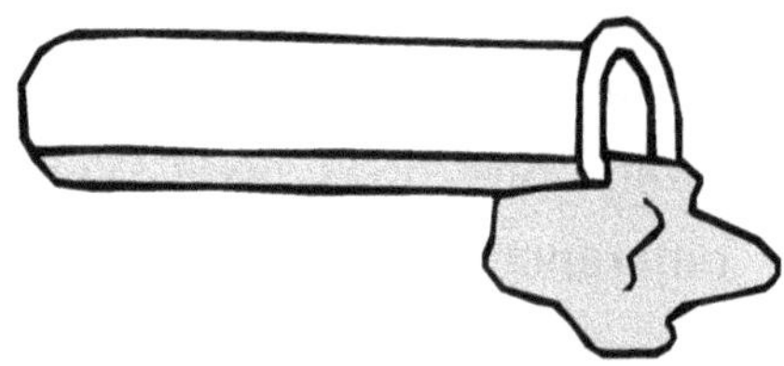

SCIENCE LEARNING STANDARD F 2

Essential Skill Activity:

Students become aware of global issues by your challenging their misconceptions such as anything natural is not a pollutant, oceans are limitless resources and humans are indestructible as a species.

What we learned today...

____

____

____

____

____

____

____

Family Science Night

Number of People: 2+ Time: Varies

Grade Level **7**

Materials: Science night activities

Description: Hurricanes in bottles and volcano-like eruptions keep kids and parents traveling from classroom to classroom during your school's Family Science Night. One classroom is glowing, while another emits a strange odor. The result of such an event is a crop of budding Einsteins. Take *What we learned today...* on some of these activities and try them at home.

SCIENCE LEARNING STANDARD A 2

Essential Skill Activity:

Scientific progress is made by asking meaningful questions and conducting careful investigations.

Kitchen Science

Number of People: 2+ Time: Varies

Grade Level **7**

Materials: Sponge, food coloring, potato, water

Description: Kitchens are a great place for science fun. Watch a sponge soak up water. Mix colors using food coloring. Put half a potato in water and place it on the window sill. Change a recipe to see what happens. These are all fantastic kitchen experiments. Just don't let your child do anything involving the word "dynamite."

SCIENCE LEARNING STANDARD A 2

Essential Skill Activity:

Teens learn that scientific progress is made by asking meaningful questions and conducting careful investigations.

Bird Feeder II

Number of People: 2   Time: Hour

Grade Level **7**

Materials: Bird feeder

Description: A bird feeder outside your window allows you and your child the chance to watch many varieties of birds. Learn about the birds in your area. Have your child keep a diary of the life cycle of one of his favorite birds. When do they reproduce? How long before the chicks are born? How long until the babies fly? How long do they stay in the nest? Where do they go when they are grown? Will he see them next season?

SCIENCE LEARNING STANDARD C 1

Essential Skill Activity:

Reproduction is a characteristic of all living systems; reproduction is essential in the continuation of all species. Some species reproduce sexually while some are asexual.

Green, Green Grass

Number of People: 2   Time: Days

Grade Level **7**

Materials: Lawn, cardboard

Description: Let's do a little yard work. Have your teen/tween put a piece of cardboard on a spot on the lawn. After several days, have him lift the cardboard. What's happened to the grass? Why? What was missing? What will bring the color back?

SCIENCE LEARNING STANDARD C 4

Essential Skill Activity:

For ecosystems the major source of energy is sunlight. The failure of any part can affect the entire system.

STARt your plants out right.

Hot House

Number of People: 2 Time: Days

Grade Level **7**

Materials: Lawn, wide mouth jar

Description: Have your child place a wide mouth jar over a patch of grass for a few days in the spring. What happens? Why? The glass creates a greenhouse to hold in the moisture. How could you help some of your new plants grow a bit faster?

SCIENCE LEARNING STANDARD C 4

Essential Skill Activity:

Students learn about the structures and processes by which flowering plants generate pollen, ovules, seeds, and fruit.

What we learned today...

I'd reSTARt everyone's coffee after this experiment.

Coffee Leftovers

Number of People: 2 Time: Several Days Grade Level **8**

Materials: Coffee, three cups

Description: Don't throw your old coffee away. Give your child three cups of your recycled coffee grounds. Put one cup on the window sill in the sun, one cup in the refrigerator, and one cup in a dark cupboard. Watch what happens. Why? I suggest making a fresh pot of coffee to drink before you have any discussions about the older cups of coffee.

SCIENCE LEARNING STANDARD A 2

Essential Skill Activity:

Students learn to recognize the relationships between explanation and evidence.

What we learned today...

Kitchen Matters

Grade Level 

Number of People: 2 Time: 20 minutes

Materials: Six glasses, a spoon, water, pencil

Description: Some night when you're doing the dishes, set out three glasses. In one glass put a spoon, fill another with water, and put nothing in the third. Ask your teen if she can see each item in the glasses. Put the contents of each glass into a fourth glass. Do the items change shape? Try putting a pencil through the spoon, the water, and then the air in the glass. Can you do it? Does each item fill the glass it's in? Give each item a name – solid, liquid or gas. Molecules in the solid form move slower than in the liquid form and both are slower than gas. Find other "slow" and "fast" molecules in your kitchen matter.

SCIENCE LEARNING STANDARD B 1

Essential Skill Activity:

Students learn the states of matter (solid, liquid, or gas) depend on molecular motion.

Straw Bubbles II

Grade Level 8

Number of People: 2 Time: 10 Minutes

Materials: Drink, straw

Description: Kids love to blow air through straws. Next time, instead of asking them to stop, ask them what's happening. What makes the bubbles? Why do the bubbles go up instead of down? What happens when the bubbles get to the top of the water? What are the bubbles made of? What type of matter is air? What type of matter is water? How do the molecules move?

SCIENCE LEARNING STANDARD B 1

Essential Skill Activity:

Kids learn to observe and measure characteristics and properties and simple chemical changes of pure substances.

Clean Up Your Pennies

Number of People: 2 Time: 30 minutes

Grade Level **8**

Materials: Jar, ¼ c. vinegar, pinch of salt, 15 copper pennies, iron nail, scouring powder

Description:Have your child clean an iron nail with scouring powder and set it aside. Help him put a 1/4 cup of vinegar and a pinch of salt in a jar. Add copper pennies. Let the jar sit for a few minutes. Drop the clean nail into the mixture of vinegar, salt, and copper pennies. Talk about what happened. Do either of you know why? Look up copper acetate on the Internet in case you don't know.

SCIENCE LEARNING STANDARD B 1

Essential Skill Activity:

Chemical reactions are processes in which atoms are rearranged into different combinations of molecules.

Science Cakes

Number of People: 2 Time: An hour

Grade Level **8**

Materials: Ingredients to make a cake

Description: Bake a few cakes from scratch. Put all the correct ingredients in one cake. In the others, leave one ingredient out– the egg, the oil, the baking powder. What happens to each cake? What chemical reaction is required from each ingredient? You might want to eat only one of the cakes.

SCIENCE LEARNING STANDARD B 1

Essential Skill Activity:

Students know reactant atoms and molecules interact to form products with different chemical properties.

You won't ever STARve when you know about how science and food go together.

Solutions

Number of People: 2 Time: 15 minutes Grade Level **8**

Materials: Glass, tablespoon, water, sugar, teaspoon

Description: A solution is a homogeneous mixture composed of two or more substances. There are three types of solutions—gas, liquid and solid. For example, water is a liquid solution of hydrogen (gas) and oxygen (gas). Let your teen dissolve a tablespoon of sugar (solid) in a glass of water (liquid). Have him stir until there are no grains of sugar in the glass. Have him taste a teaspoon of the mixture at the top of the glass. Then have him pour out half of the glass. Have him taste a teaspoon of the mixture from the middle of the glass. Is there a difference in the taste? Have him describe a solution in his own words.

SCIENCE LEARNING STANDARD B 1

Essential Skill Activity:

Students know reactant atoms and molecules interact to form products with different chemical properties.

What we learned today...

Science experiments bring about such STARtling results sometimes.

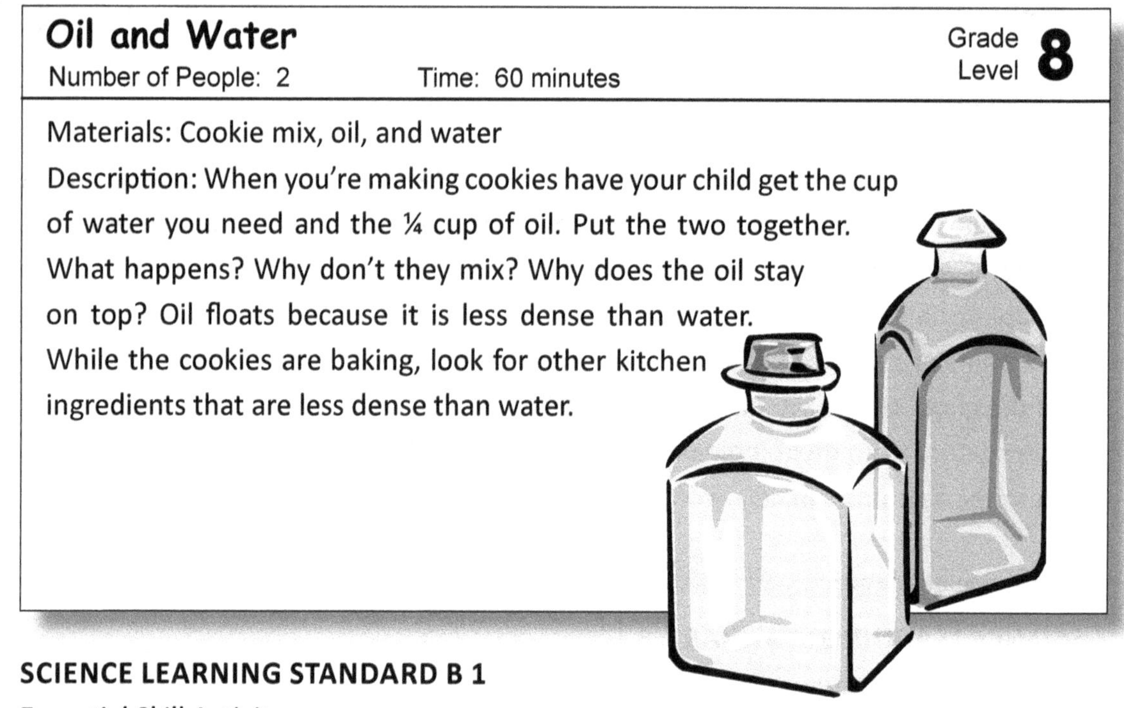

Oil and Water

Number of People: 2 Time: 60 minutes

Grade Level **8**

Materials: Cookie mix, oil, and water

Description: When you're making cookies have your child get the cup of water you need and the ¼ cup of oil. Put the two together. What happens? Why don't they mix? Why does the oil stay on top? Oil floats because it is less dense than water. While the cookies are baking, look for other kitchen ingredients that are less dense than water.

SCIENCE LEARNING STANDARD B 1

Essential Skill Activity:

Students learn the idea of atoms explains the conservation of matter.

What we learned today...

Making Rust

Number of People: 2 Time: Varies

Grade Level **8**

Materials: Steel wool, jar, saucer, water

Description: Let's make rust. Have your teen put a piece of steel wool at the bottom of a narrow jar. (Make sure you rinse out any soap that may be in your steel wool first.) Fill a saucer with water. Place the jar upside down on the saucer. Put the saucer in a safe place. Check the steel wool and the saucer every few days. Let him replace the water as it evaporates. When a red substance begins forming on the steel wool, you have created ferric oxide. Can he explain what is happening? If he can't, have him check the Internet to find out.

SCIENCE LEARNING STANDARD B 1

Essential Skill Activity:

In chemical reactions the number of atoms stays the same no matter how they are arranged, so their total mass stays the same.

Marshmallow Molecules

Number of People: 2 Time: 30+ Minutes

Grade Level 

Materials: Marshmallows both white and colored, toothpicks, juice, baking soda, spoon

Description: You and your child can make a water molecule model using marshmallows. One large marshmallow can represent the oxygen atom. Two small colored marshmallows can act as two hydrogen atoms. Connect them with the toothpicks. Place one small marshmallow at twelve o'clock and one small marshmallow at seven o'clock. Salt molecules are even easier. NaCl looks like one small marshmallow attached to one large marshmallow. Are there others you and your child can make?

SCIENCE LEARNING STANDARD B 1

Essential Skill Activity:

Students can create an example of elements with a specific number of protons in the nucleus and show the number of neutrons in the nucleus.

Roller Movement

Number of People: 2 Time: 10 minutes

Grade Level 

Materials: Metal tray, salt, soda can

Description: Is it better to push or to roll? Help your child spread salt on a tray. Put a soda can on one end and push the can across the salted tray. Redistribute the salt. Now put the soda can on its side and roll the can across the salt. Which way was easier? Why? Which way would you use to move other items?

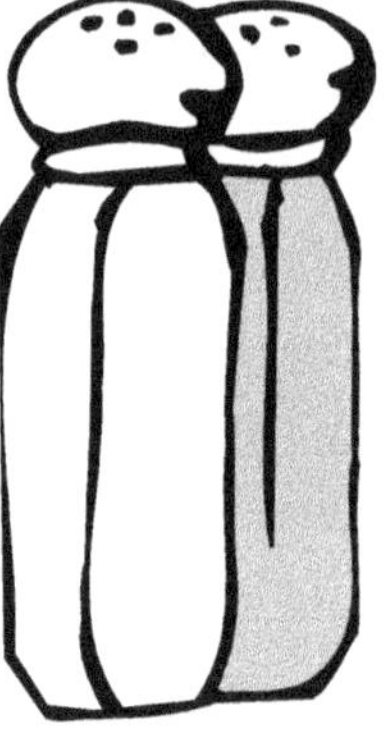

SCIENCE LEARNING STANDARDS B 2 & B 3

Essential Skill Activity:

Students learn how to identify separately the two or more forces that are acting on a single object.

Popcorn Science

Number of People: 2 Time: 15 minutes

Grade Level 

Materials: Popping corn, corn popper, oil

Description: Have your child measure out ¼ cup of popcorn. Pop the corn in the oil over a hot burner. Have your child measure what is popped. Why the difference? What happened? What would happen to ½ cup? A whole cup? Enjoy the popcorn with butter and a movie.

SCIENCE LEARNING STANDARD B 3

Essential Skill Activity:

Students know chemical reactions usually liberate heat or absorb heat.

Frozen Solid

Number of People: 2 Time: Hour+

Grade Level **8**

Materials: Small plastic or glass bottle, water, aluminum foil

Description: Show your teen how water changes shape. Fill a small bottle to the brim with water. Make a loose fitting cap with a piece of aluminum foil. Place the bottle in the freezer standing up so it doesn't spill. Leave the bottle until the water has frozen completely. What's happened? What would happen if you put a can of soda in the freezer? What could happen to your home's water pipes in the winter?

SCIENCE LEARNING STANDARD B 3

Essential Skill Activity:

Students learn that some physical processes include freezing and boiling, in which a material changes form with no chemical reaction.

What we learned today...

You are becoming a megaSTAR scientist.

Cabbage Experiments Grade Level **8**

Number of People: 2 Time: 20 minutes

Materials: Two plastic cups, red cabbage, hot water, lemon juice, baking soda, spoon

Description: One evening while making dinner, put some red cabbage in a plastic cup. Add hot water. The water will turn blue. You now have an acid-base indicator. Separate the blue water into two cups. Let your child put lemon juice in one and baking soda in the other. What happens? Why? Once more we have science in the kitchen.

SCIENCE LEARNING Standard B 3

Essential Skill Activity:

Students learn how chemical reactions affect atoms.

What we learned today...

Moving Molecules

Number of People: 2 Time: 20 Minutes

Grade Level **8**

Materials: Glass of hot water, glass of cold water, food coloring

Description:Let your teen show you how molecules move. Have her put two drops of food coloring into a glass of hot water and two drops of food coloring into a glass of cold water. Using a stopwatch (or a watch with a second hand), time how long it takes for the water in each glass to become one color. Notice how the faster moving molecules in the hot water dissipate the color faster. The speed with which molecules move in specific substances helps scientists classify those substances on the periodic table.

SCIENCE LEARNING STANDARD B 3

Essential Skill Activity:

Students learn that substances can be classified by their properties, including their melting temperature, density, hardness, and thermal and electrical conductivity.

Layering Liquids

Number of People: 2 Time: 30 minutes

Grade Level **8**

Materials: 1 c. water, 1 c. molasses, 1 c. cooking oil, tall glass, a pitcher, spoon, juice, baking soda, spoon

Description: Have your teen carefully pour each of the above liquids one at a time over a spoon into a tall glass jar. What happens? Which of the liquids has the highest density? Float a few household items in the liquids and see what happens. Try a cork, a slice of apple, a grape, or a paperclip. What happens? Have him describe what is happening.

SCIENCE LEARNING STANDARD B 3

Essential Skill Activity:

Students learn that a buoyant force on an object in a fluid is an upward force equal to the weight of the fluid the object has displaced.

Create your own playbook activities!

Science
Number of People: Time:
Grade Level

Materials:
Description:

SCIENCE LEARNING STANDARD

Science
Number of People: Time:
Grade Level

Materials:
Description:

SCIENCE LEARNING STANDARD

Create your own playbook activities!

Science

Number of People: Time:

Grade Level

Materials:

Description:

SCIENCE LEARNING STANDARD

Science

Number of People: Time:

Grade Level

Materials:

Description:

SCIENCE LEARNING STANDARD

HISTORY

6 – 8

Parent Playbook Activities

Want to add your favorite activity to the next Parent Playbook? Use the convenient form in the back of this book or contact the publisher at:

www.familyfriendlyschools.com • www.engagepress.com

By Dr. Joni Samples **History Learning Standards**

STANDARDS HISTORY/SOCIAL STUDIES
Grades 6-8

The purpose of the History/Social Studies Learning Standards is to enable all students to achieve an understanding of history. The following standards for History/Social Studies are a compilation of standards being used in districts across the nation.

The K-8 standards are a continuous roadmap of knowledge building one skill upon another. This roadmap tells us how to get to the final destination.

The History/Social Studies Learning Standards provide expectations for the development of student understanding and ability over the course of their K-8 education.

We have listed History/Social Studies Learning Standards on the following pages to help you understand how each activity connects to each standard. Also included are the Historical Thinking Standards to help create thoughtful reflection of historic events.

History
Grades 6-8

Standards in history make explicit the goals that all students should have the opportunity to acquire. In history, standards are of two types:

1. Historical thinking skills. Being able to think enables students to evaluate evidence, compare and analyze, be able to explain, and put together sound historical arguments and evaluate and make informed decisions.

2. Historical understandings. This defines what students should know about the history of their nation and of the world. Students learn this through studying the social, political, scientific/technological, economic, and cultural (philosophical/religious/aesthetic) records. These records also provide students the historical perspectives required to analyze contemporary issues and problems confronting citizens today.

Both the World and United States Standards are printed for your information as well as the Historical Thinking Standards.

A NOTE ABOUT THE HISTORY SECTION

The standards in History look very different from other standards listed in this Playbook. Why? Well, the study of history involves much more than the passive absorption of facts, dates, names, and places. History is in essence a process of reasoning based on evidence from the past. This reasoning must be grounded in the careful gathering, weighing and sifting of information such as names, dates, places, ideas, and events. However, the process does not stop here. Real historical understanding requires students to think through cause-and-effect relationships, to reach sound historical interpretations, and to conduct historical inquiries and research leading to the knowledge on which informed decisions in contemporary life can be based.

History itself is a highly integrative field, engaging students in studies not only of the people and of events in their community, state, nation, and world, but opening as well the study of the geographic places in which these events occurred. It includes the ideas, beliefs, and values that influenced how people acted in their daily lives; the rules, laws, and institutions they established and lived by; the oral traditions and the literature, music, art, architecture, and dance they created; and the technological and scientific developments they invented, or adopted, in their quest to improve daily life. In short, studies in history necessarily include geographic, economic, political, social, and scientific studies, as well as studies in the arts.

Historical thinking and understanding do not develop independently of one another. Historical thinking skills enable students to evaluate evidence, develop comparative and causal analyses, interpret the historical record, and construct sound historical arguments and perspectives on which informed decisions in contemporary life can be based. Historical understandings define what students should know about the history of their nation and of the world. These understandings also provide students the historical perspectives required to analyze contemporary issues and problems confronting citizens today.

In the History/Social Studies section of your Parent Playbook the History/Social Studies Learning Standard is listed below the activity. Parent Playbook, the History/Social Studies Learning Standard and the Thinking Standard are listed by number ... and you may refer back to the beginning of the chapter for the actual standard.

HISTORY LEARNING STANDARDS
Grades 6-8

Standards in history make explicit the goals that all students should have the opportunity to acquire. In history, standards are of two types:

1. Historical thinking skills. Being able to think enables students to evaluate evidence, compare and analyze, be able to explain, and put together sound historical arguments and evaluate and make informed decisions.

2. Historical understandings. This defines what students should know about the history of their nation and of the world. They learn this through studying the social, political, scientific/technological, economic, and cultural (philosophical/religious/aesthetic) records. They also provide students the historical perspectives required to analyze contemporary issues and problems confronting citizens today.

Both the World and United States Standards are printed for your information as well as the Historical Thinking Standards for your information.

WORLD HISTORY LEARNING STANDARD
Grades 6-8

Era 1: The beginning of Human Society
Standard 1: The biological and cultural processes that gave rise to the earliest human communities
Standard 2: The processes that led to the emergence of agricultural societies around the world

Era 2: Early Civilizations and the emergence of Pastoral Peoples (4000-1000 BCE)
Standard 1: The major characteristics of civilization and how civilizations emerged in Mesopotamia, Egypt, and the Indus valley
Standard 2: How agrarian societies spread and new states emerged in the third and second millennia BCE
Standard 3: The political, social, and cultural consequences of population movements and militarization in Eurasia in the second millennium BCE
Standard 4: Major trends in Eurasia and Africa from 4000-1000 BCE

Era 3: Classical Traditions, Major Religions, and Giant Empires (1000 BCE – 300 CE)
Standard 1: Innovation and change from 1000-600 BCE horses, ships, iron, and monotheistic faith
Standard 2: The emergence of Aegean civilization and how interrelations developed among peoples of the eastern Mediterranean and Southwest Asia, 600-200 BCE
Standard 3: How major religions and large-scale empires arose in the Mediterranean basin, China, and India, 500 BCE - 300 CE
Standard 4: The development of early agrarian civilizations in Mesoamerica
Standard 5: Major global trends from 1000 BCE - 300 CE

Era 4: Expanding Zones of Exchange and Encounter (300-1000 CE)
Standard 1: Imperial crises and their aftermath, 300-700 CE
Standard 2: Causes and consequences of the rise of Islamic civilization in the 7th-10th centuries
Standard 3: Major developments in East Asia and Southeast Asia in the era of the Tang dynasty, 600-900 CE
Standard 4: The search for political, social, and cultural redefinition in Europe, 500-1000 CE
Standard 5: The development of agricultural societies and new states in tropical Africa and Oceania
Standard 6: The rise of centers of civilization in Mesoamerica and Andean South America in the first millennium CE

Standard 7: Major global trends from 300-1000 CE

Era 5: Intensified Hemispheric Interactions (1000-1500 CE)
Standard 1: The maturing of an interregional system of communication, trade, and cultural exchange in an era of Chinese economic power and Islamic expansion
Standard 2: The redefining of European society and culture, 1000-1300 CE
Standard 3: The rise of the Mongol empire and its consequences for Eurasian peoples, 1200-1350 CE
Standard 4: The growth of states, towns, and trade in Sub-Saharan Africa between the 11th and 15th centuries
Standard 5: Patterns of crisis and recovery in Afro-Eurasia, 1300-1450 CE
Standard 6: The expansion of states and civilizations in the Americas, 1000-1500 CE
Standard 7: Major global trends from 1000-1500 CE

Era 6: Emergence of First Global Age (1450-1770)
Standard 1: How the transoceanic interlinking of all major regions of the world from 1450-1600 led to global transformations
Standard 2: How European society experienced political, economic, and cultural transformations in an age of global intercommunication, 1450-1750
Standard 3: How large territorial empires dominated much of Eurasia between the 16th and 18th centuries
Standard 4: Economic, political, and cultural interrelations among peoples of Africa, Europe, and the Americas, 1500-1750
Standard 5: Transformations in Asian societies in the era of European expansion
Standard 6: Major global trends from 1450-1770

Era 7: Age of Revolution (1875-1914)
Standard 1: The causes and consequences of political revolution in the 18th and early 19th century
Standard 2: The causes and consequences of the agricultural and industrial revolution (1700-1850)
Standard 3: Transformation of Eurasian societies in an era of global trade and rising European power (1750-1870)
Standard 4: Patterns of nationalism, State-building and social reform in Europe and Americas (1830-1914)
Standard 5: Patterns of global change in the era of Western military and economic domination (1800-1914)

Standard 6: Major global trends from 1750-1914

Era 8: A Half Century of Crisis and Achievement (1900-1945)
Standard 1: The causes and consequences of political revolutions in the late 18th and early 19th centuries
Standard 2: The causes and consequences of the agricultural and industrial revolutions, 1700-1850
Standard 3: The transformation of Eurasian societies in an era of global trade and rising European power, 1750-1870
Standard 4: Patterns of nationalism, state-building, and social reform in Europe and the Americas, 1830-1914
Standard 5: Patterns of global change in the era of Western military and economic domination, 1800-1914
Standard 6: Major global trends from 1750-1914

Era 9: 20th Century Since 1945-Promises and Paradoxes
Standard 1: How post-World War II reconstruction occurred, new international power relations took shape, and colonial empires broke up
Standard 2: The search for community, stability, and peace in and interdependent world
Standard 3: Major global trends since World War II

Era 10: World History across the Eras
Standard 1: Long-term change and recurring patterns in world history

UNITED STATES HISTORY LEARNING ST ANDARD Grades 6-8

Era 1: Three Worlds Meet (Beginnings to 1620)
Standard 1: Comparative characteristics of societies in the Americas, Western Europe, and Western Africa that increasingly interacted after 1450
Standard 2: How early European exploration and colonization resulted in cultural and ecological interactions among previously unconnected peoples

Era 2: Colonization and Settlement (1585-1763)
Standard 1: Why the Americas attracted Europeans, why they brought enslaved Africans to their colonies, and how Europeans struggled for control of North America and the Caribbean
Standard 2: How political, religious, and social institutions emerged in the English colonies
Standard 3: How the values and institutions of European economic life took root in the colonies, and how slavery reshaped European and African life in the Americas

Era 3: Revolution and the New Nation (1754-1820's)
Standard 1: The causes of the American Revolution, the ideas and interests involved in forging the revolutionary movement, and the reasons for the American victory
Standard 2: The impact of the American Revolution on politics, economy, and society
Standard 3: The institutions and practices of government created during the Revolution and how they were revised between 1787 and 1815 to create the foundation of the American political system based on the U.S. Constitution and the Bill of Rights

Era 4: Expansion and Reform (1801-1861)
Standard 1: United States territorial expansion between 1801 and 1861, and how it affected relations with external powers and Native Americans
Standard 2: How the industrial revolution, increasing immigration, the rapid expansion of slavery, and the westward movement changed the lives of Americans and led toward regional tensions
Standard 3: The extension, restriction, and reorganization of political democracy after 1800
Standard 4: The sources and character of cultural, religious, and social reform movements in the antebellum period

Era 5: Civil War and Reconstruction (1850-1877)
Standard 1: The causes of the Civil War
Standard 2: The course and character of the Civil War and its effects on the American people
Standard 3: How various reconstruction plans succeeded or failed

Era 6: The Development of the Industrial United States (1870-1900)
Standard 1: How the rise of corporations, heavy industry, and mechanized farming transformed the American people
Standard 2: Massive immigration after 1870 and how new social patterns, conflicts, and ideas of national unity developed amid growing cultural diversity
Standard 3: The rise of the American Labor Movement and how political issues reflected social and economic changes
Standard 4: Federal Indian policy and United States foreign policy after the Civil War

Era 7: The Emergence of Modern America (1890-1930)
Standard 1: How Progressives and others addressed problems of industrial capitalism, urbanization, and political corruption
Standard 2: The changing role of the United States in world affairs through World War I
Standard 3: How the United States changed from the end of World War I to the eve of the Great Depression

Era 8: The Great Depression and World War II (1929-1945)
Standard 1: The causes of the Great Depression and how it affected American society
Standard 2: How the New Deal addressed the Great Depression, transformed American federalism, and initiated the welfare state
Standard 3: The causes and course of World War II, the character of the war at home and abroad, and its reshaping of the U.S. role in world affairs

Era 9: Postwar United States (1945 to early 1970s)
Standard 1: the economic boom and social transformation of postwar United States
Standard 2: How the Cold War and conflicts in Korea and Vietnam influenced domestic and international politics
Standard 3: Domestic policies after World War II
Standard 4: The struggle for racial and gender equality and the extension of civil liberties

Era 10: Contemporary United States (1968 to the present)
Standard 1: Recent developments in foreign and domestic politics
Standard 2: Economic, social, and cultural developments in contemporary United States

HISTORICAL THINKING STANDARDS
Grades 6-8

STANDARD 1
The student thinks chronologically: Therefore, the student is able to:

A. Distinguish between past, present, and future time.
B. Identify the temporal structure of a historical narrative or story: its beginning, middle, and end (the latter defined as the outcome of a particular beginning).
C. Establish temporal order in constructing their [students'] own historical narratives: working forward from some beginning through its development, to some end or outcome; working backward from some issue, problem, or event to explain its origins and its development over time.
D. Measure and calculate calendar time by days, weeks, months, years, decades, centuries and millennia, from fixed points of the calendar system: BC (before Christ) and AD (Anno Domini, "in the year of our Lord") in the Gregorian calendar and the contemporary secular designation for these same dates, BCE (before the Common Era) and CE (in the Common Era); and compare with the fixed points of other calendar systems such as the Roman (753BC, the founding of the city of Rome) and the Muslim (622 AD, the hegira).
E. Interpret data presented in time lines by designating appropriate equidistant intervals of time and recording events according to the temporal order in which they occurred.
F. Reconstruct patterns of historical succession and duration in which historical developments have unfolded, and apply them to explain historical continuity and change.
G. Compare alternative models for periodization by identifying the organizing principles on which each is based.

STANDARD 2:
The student comprehends a variety of historical sources: Therefore, the student is able to:

A. Identify the author or source of the historical document or narrative.
B. Reconstruct the literal meaning of a historical passage by identifying who was involved, what happened, where it happened, what events led to these developments, and what consequences or outcomes followed.
C. Identify the central question(s) the historical narrative addresses and the purpose, perspective, or point of view from which it has been constructed.
D. Differentiate between historical facts and historical interpretations but acknowledge that the two are related; that the facts the historian reports are selected and reflect therefore the historian's judgment of what is most significant about the past.
E. Read historical narratives imaginatively, taking into account what the narrative reveals of the

humanity of the individuals and groups involved – their probable values, outlook, motives, hopes, fears, strengths, and weaknesses.

F. Appreciate historical perspectives – the ability (a) describing the past on its own terms, through the eyes and experiences of those who were there, as revealed through their literature, diaries, letters, debates, arts, artifacts, and the like; (b) considering the historical context in which the event unfolded – the values, outlook, options, and contingencies of that time and place; and (c) avoiding "present-mindedness," judging the past solely in terms of present-day norms and values.

G. Draw upon data in historical maps in order to obtain or clarify information on the geographic setting in which the historical event occurred, its relative and absolute location, the distances and directions involved, the natural and man-made features of the place, and critical relationships in the spatial distributions of those features and the historical event occurring there.

H. Utilize visual and mathematical data presented in graphs, including charts, tables, pie and bar graphs, flow charts, Venn diagrams, and other graphic organizers to clarify, illustrate, or elaborate upon information presented in the historical narrative.

I. Draw upon the visual, literary, and musical sources including: (a) photographs, paintings, cartoons, and architectural drawings; (b) novels, poetry, and plays; and (c) folk, popular, and classical music, to clarify, illustrate, or elaborate upon information presented in the historical narrative.

STANDARD 3:

The student engages in historical analysis and interpretation: therefore, the student is able to:

A. Compare and contrast differing sets of ideas, values, personalities, behaviors, and institutions by identifying likenesses and differences.

B. Consider multiple perspectives of various peoples in the past by demonstrating their differing motives, beliefs, interests, hopes, and fears.

C. Analyze cause-and-effect relationships bearing in mind multiple causation including (a) the importance of the individual in history; (b) the influence of ideas, human interests, and beliefs; and (c) the role of chance, the accidental and the irrational.

D. Draw comparisons across eras and regions in order to define enduring issues as well as large-scale or long-term developments that transcend regional and temporal boundaries.

E. Distinguish between unsupported expressions of opinion and informed hypotheses grounded in historical evidence.

F. Compare competing historical narratives.

G. Challenge arguments of historical inevitability by formulating examples of historical contingency, of how different choices could have led to different consequences.

H. Hold interpretations of history as tentative, subject to changes as new information is uncovered, new voices heard, and new interpretations broached.

I. Evaluate major debates among historians concerning alternative interpretations of the past.

J. Hypothesize the influence of the past, including both the limitations and opportunities made possible by past decisions.

STANDARD 4:

The student conducts historical research: Therefore, the student is able to:

A. Formulate historical questions from encounters with historical documents, eyewitness accounts, letters, diaries, artifacts, photos, historical sites, art, architecture, and other records from the past.
B. Obtain historical data from a variety of sources, including: library and museum collections, historic sites, historical photos, journals, diaries, eyewitness accounts, newspapers, and the like; documentary films, oral testimony from living witnesses, censuses, tax records, city directories, statistical compilations, and economic indicators.
C. Interrogate historical data by uncovering the social, political, and economic context in which it was created; testing the data source for its credibility, authority, authenticity, internal consistency and completeness; and detecting and evaluating bias, distortion, and propaganda by omission, suppression, or invention of facts.
D. Identify the gaps in the available records and marshal contextual knowledge and perspectives of the time and place in order to elaborate imaginatively upon the evidence, fill in the gaps deductively, and construct a sound historical interpretation.
E. Employ quantitative analysis in order to explore such topics as changes in family size and composition, migration patterns, wealth distribution, and changes in the economy.
F. Support interpretations with historical evidence in order to construct closely reasoned arguments rather than facile opinions.

STANDARD 5:

The student engages in historical issues-analysis and decision making: Therefore, the student is able to:

A. Identify issues and problems in the past and analyze the interests, values, perspectives, and points of view of those involved in the situation.
B. Marshal evidence of antecedent circumstances and current factors contributing to contemporary problems and alternative courses of action.
C. Identify relevant historical antecedents and differentiate from those that are inappropriate and irrelevant to contemporary issues.
D. Evaluate alternative courses of action, keeping in mind the information available at the time, in terms of ethical considerations, the interests of those affected by the decision, and the long- and short-term consequences of each.
E. Formulate a position or course of action on an issue by identifying the nature of the problem, analyzing the underlying factors contributing to the problem, and choosing a plausible solution from a choice of carefully evaluated options.
F. Evaluate the implementation of a decision by analyzing the interests it served; estimating the position, power, and priority of each player involved; assessing the ethical dimensions of the decision; and evaluating its costs and benefits from a variety of perspectives.

Who's Who and What's What

Number of People: 2 Time: 20 minutes

Grade Level 

Materials: History/Social Studies book, paper, and pencil

Description: There are lots of people and events to learn about in middle school history/social studies. We used to make lists of the people and events in the chapters our kids were studying. During the evening, we'd go through the list and see how many people our kids knew. At first, there weren't many. By Friday, they could tell us about 90% of the list.

HISTORICAL THINKING STANDARD 1A

Analyze cause and effect of relationships

Homo Sapiens Uncovered

Number of People: 2 Time: Hour+

Grade Level 

Materials: Internet, history book, colored pens and paper

Description: Have your child create a graphic design to show the ancestry of Homo Sapiens. Have her name the ancestors of our species and the innovations of the various groups of ancestors. Start at the earliest recorded time and work up through the hunter-gatherer societies. This can get as basic or as elaborate as you choose. Just be sure she includes the use of tools and fire as part of the display.

WORLD HISTORY LEARNING STANDARD ERA 1, STANDARDS 1 & 2

HISTORICAL THINKING STANDARD 1 A

STARt by identifying where you are on your map.

New maps for Old: Paleolithic Times Grade Level **6**

Number of People: 2 Time: 30 minutes

Materials: Maps – both current and from previous centuries

Description: There are many places to discover when learning history/social studies. A map is helpful, but the names on the map may be different now than they were centuries ago. Ask your child to identify geographic areas from the Paleolithic era. Find out who lived there and what their world was like.

WORLD HISTORY LEARNING STANDARD ERA 2, STANDARDS 1 & 2
HISTORICAL THINKING STANDARD 2 G

What we learned today...

How many upSTARt countries can you find that have disappeared after a short time or even centuries.

New maps for Old: Mesopotamia, Egypt and Kush

Grade Level **6**

Number of People: 2   Time: 30 minutes

Materials: Maps – both current and from previous centuries, the Internet for research

Description: Ask your child to identify the geographic areas of Mesopotamia, Egypt, and Kush. Who lived there? Who were the leaders? What did they do? Why are they important today? Look at a current map and compare it with an ancient map. Are the names of these areas the same or different?

WORLD HISTORY LEARNING STANDARD ERA 2, STANDARDS 1 & 2
HISTORICAL THINKING STANDARD 2 G

What we learned today...

Trivial Pursuit

Number of People: 2 Time: Several hours

Grade Level 

Materials: Paper and pencil, research sources-history book, Internet

Description: Have your child create trivial pursuit questions about the Ancient Hebrews. Choose categories such as: geography, politics, economics, religion, and social structure. Have her research each of the areas and create some questions. See if she can stump the rest of the family. You can use trivial pursuit for just about any subject. There's trivia everywhere.

WORLD HISTORY LEARNING STANDARD ERA 2, STANDARDS 1, 2, 3, & 4
HISTORICAL THINKING STANDARDS, 4 A & B

Greek Days

Number of People: 2 Time: Hour+

Grade Level 

Materials: Paper and pencil, research sources – history book, Internet

Description: How many Greek mythological figures can you remember? On a piece of paper, brainstorm with your child all the mythological figures that come to your minds. Who were they? What did they do? Do you know their symbol? Then, research on the Internet or in the library to see if you were correct and find out more. Who turned out to be a Roman mythological figure rather than Greek? Continue adding to your list as you find mythological figures you find interesting. Who are the most interesting to your child? Why?

WORLD HISTORY LEARNING STANDARD ERA 3, STANDARDS 1 & 2
HISTORICAL THINKING STANDARD 4 B

War Journal

Number of People: 2 Time: Hour+

Grade Level 

Materials: Paper and pencil, research sources – history book, Internet

Description: Have your child pretend he is a person living in Athens during the Persian and Peloponnesian Wars. He may need to do some research in book or on the Internet to see what it was like at that time. Have him write an account of what is happening around him. What were the causes of the war? How was his life changed? How did the war end? How might all of it been avoided?

WORLD HISTORY LEARNING STANDARD ERA 3, STANDARDS 3, 4, & 5
HISTORICAL THINKING STANDARDS 5 A

New Maps for Old: The Roman Empire

Number of People: 2 Time: 30 Minutes

Grade Level 

Materials: Maps – both current and from previous centuries, Internet for research
Description: There are many places to discover when learning history/social studies. A map is helpful, but the names may be different now than they were centuries ago. Ask your child to identify the geographic area of the Roman Empire. Why was this area so large? Who were the leaders that made it so? What were the major contributions of the people living there? Ask your child to identify the ancient names and find out what they are named today.

WORLD HISTORY LEARNING STANDARD ERA 4, STANDARD 4
HISTORICAL THINKING STANDARD 3 C & D

Buddha STARted a religion with his meditation and enlightenment.

Rub Buddha's Belly

Number of People: 2+ Time: Hour+

Grade Level **6**

Materials: Internet for research

Description: There is a Mongolian bar-b-que restaurant in my town where a large statue of Buddha lives. My children remember the restaurant not for the food, but for the Buddha. They have asked who, what, and why several times. See if there's a local place in your home town that would raise these questions. The food is usually good and it allows you to research the influence of Buddhism in India and Central Asia. What is the influence in the United States?

WORLD HISTORY LEARNING STANDARD ERA 5, STANDARD 3
HISTORICAL THINKING STANDARD 2 B

What we learned today...

Romans outSTARred everyone else in their day!

Who Was There?
Number of People: 2+ Time: Hour+

Grade Level **7**

Materials: Paper and pencil, research sources – history book, Internet

Description: Have your child pretend to interview a Roman citizen who lived during the Roman Empire. You can help by being the Roman citizen so you'll want to find some answers to the questions your interviewer will ask. The Internet or his textbooks are great helps. What would the citizen remember about the Roman Empire? Where did the citizen live? What job did he hold? What was happening in art, architecture, and philosophy at the time? What were the strengths of the Empire in the citizen's opinion? What were its weaknesses? What would the citizen have done differently if he had been in charge of Rome?

WORLD HISTORY LEARNING STANDARD ERA 2, STANDARDS 1, 2, 3, & 4
HISTORICAL THINKING STANDARD 5 F

What we learned today...

New Maps for Old: Medieval Europe

Grade Level **7**

Number of People: 2 Time: 30 Minutes

Materials: Maps – both current and from previous centuries, Internet for research

Description: There are many places to discover when learning history/social studies. A map is helpful, but the names may be different now than they were centuries ago. Ask your child to identify the geographic area of Medieval Europe. What were the location, topography, and climate like? Where were the names of major waterways and what type of vegetation did the people of Medieval Europe depend on? How did the land support the feudal system? What are the old names of the area and what do we call them today?

WORLD HISTORY LEARNING STANDARD ERA 4, STANDARDS 1 & 4
HISTORICAL THINKING STANDARD 2 G

Time Traveler

Grade Level **7**

Number of People: 2 Time:30+ minutes

Materials: Paper and pencil, research sources – history book, Internet

Description: Have your child pretend to be a time traveler. Ask her to pick a famous person from a time period they are studying. Ask her to pretend she's gone back in time to visit this person. What questions would she ask? What would she want to know about the time period, the country, and the language. What was happening in the rest of the world?

WORLD HISTORY LEARNING STANDARD ERAS 4, 5, & 6
HISTORICAL THINKING STANDARD 5 A & B

Marco Polo

Number of People: 2 Time: 45 Minutes

Grade Level **7**

Materials: Internet for research

Description: Kids like to play the game Marco Polo in the swimming pool. Ask your child if she knows who Marco Polo was? If not, have her research Marco Polo and his travels on the Internet. What did he do? Where did he go? Why is he important in history? The next time they play the game, she'll know whose name she's calling.

WORLD HISTORY LEARNING STANDARD ERA 5, STANDARDS 2 & 7
HISTORICAL THINKING STANDARD 4 B

Muslim Rule

Number of People: 2 Time: Hour+

Grade Level **7**

Materials: Paper and pencil, marker, or publishing program on the computer, Internet for research

Description: Have your child write headlines for a Muslim newspaper during the Middle Ages. What were the burning issues of the day? What were the products and inventions of the time? Who were the important influences? What wars were raging? Why? How is it different than a headline in a newspaper today?

WORLD HISTORY LEARNING STANDARD ERA 5, STANDARDS 3, 4, & 5
HISTORICAL THINKING STANDARD 1 A & 3 A

Ancient China may have been a bit STARK without computers and iphones.

China Sees

Number of People: 2 Time: Hour+

Grade Level **7**

Materials: Paper and pencil, research sources – history book, Internet

Description: Have your child research China during the Middle Ages on the Internet. Have him draw a picture of an invention of the era that affects us today. It could be agricultural, technological, commercial, or artistic. Have him explain why he chose the item and why he believes it is significant.

WORLD HISTORY LEARNING STANDARD ERA 5, STANDARDS 3, 4, & 5
HISTORICAL THINKING STANDARD 5 A

What we learned today...

We all learn history in bits and pieces or as I like to say, fits and STARts.

Reformation Diary

Number of People: 2 Time: 30 minutes

Grade Level **7**

Materials: Diary page

Description: Help your child research life during the Reformation in the 1400s. Have her write a diary/journal entry for a typical day. Be sure to encourage her to consider what she might have been doing during the day, what problems she might have faced, and how she would have overcome them. Have her consider what religious thought she might have followed. How would that choice have affected her life?

WORLD HISTORY LEARNING STANDARD ERA 6, STANDARD 2
HISTORICAL THINKING STANDARD 4 A

What we learned today...

What's Up?

Number of People: 2 Time: Hour+

Grade Level **7**

Materials: Paper and pencil, research sources – history book, Internet

Description: Let your child create a magazine about his world pretending as though he lived during the Scientific Revolution. He can write articles about Copernicus, Galileo, Kepler, or Newton. He can preview the newest inventions like the telescope or microscope. He can review the scientific methods of Bacon and Descartes or whatever he finds fascinating. Pictures can be created by computer, drawn, or taken from the Internet. He can make copies for his family or friends. I'm sure you'd enjoy knowing the most up to date information of the 15th century.

WORLD HISTORY LEARNING STANDARD ERA 6, STANDARD 6

HISTORICAL THINKING STANDARD 4 B

Historic Letter: War of 1812

Number of People: 2+ Time: Hour+

Grade Level **8**

Materials: Paper and ink, research sources – history book, Internet

Description: Ask your child to write you a special letter. Tell him you'd like one from the perspective of someone living during the War of 1812. What happened? Why was the war fought? With whom? What were the causes? What was the result? What bought about final peace?

NATIONAL U.S. HISTORY STANDARD ERA 4, STANDARDS 1 & 3

HISTORICAL THINKING STANDARD 5 E

Free Press

Number of People: 2 Time: Hour+

Grade Level **8**

Materials: Paper and pencil, research sources – history book, Internet

Description: Let your child imagine he is a colonist living in Massachusetts at the time of the American Revolution. Ask him to write a letter to the editor of the Boston Globe about the rights and responsibilities of a free press.

NATIONAL U.S. HISTORY STANDARD ERA 3, STANDARDS 1, 2, & 3
HISTORICAL THINKING STANDARD 5 E

Historic Letter: Continental Congress

Number of People: 2+ Time: Hour+

Grade Level **8**

Materials: Paper and ink, research sources – history book, Internet

Description: Ask your child to write you a special letter. Tell him you'd like one from someone who attended the Continental Congress. What happened? What was debated? What was decided? Who was responsible for the decisions? How would those decisions have affected his family back? Who was his favorite member of the Congress and why?

NATIONAL U.S. HISTORY STANDARD ERA 3, STANDARD 3
HISTORICAL THINKING STANDARD 3 C

STARdom is yours when you know that your present moment is your past in the next moment. Make each present moment a great one.

History Book Writer

Number of People: 2 Time: Varies Grade Level **8**

Materials: Paper, pencil, colored pencils, research sources–history book, Internet

Description: Have your child create her own history book around a particular period of time. Have her include pictures, stories, anecdotes, locations, famous people, and famous events. If she chooses the opening of the West, she could chronicle the Lewis and Clark expeditions, the Indian removal, and the settlement of the Great Plains. Her history book doesn't have to be fancy, but it should contain her research and her views of the era.

NATIONAL U.S. HISTORY STANDARD ERA 4, STANDARD 1
HISTORICAL THINKING STANDARD 2 H & I

What we learned today...

Native Americans

Number of People: 2 Time: Hour+

Grade Level **8**

Materials: Paper and pencil, research sources – history book, Internet

Description: Have your child choose one group of early Native Americans to research. Check your local library and the Internet to discover facts about the tribe you've chosen. Where did they come from? Where did they settle? How did they live? Do they have ancestors alive today? Do they live in the same location? If not, why did they move? Have your child write a story about what it was like to be a Native American during the times of our country's first few presidents.

NATIONAL U.S. HISTORY STANDARD ERA 4, STANDARDS 1 & 2 ERA 6, STANDARD 4

HISTORICAL THINKING STANDARD 2 F

What we learned today...

Thomas Jefferson Diary

Number of People: 2 Time: Hour+

Grade Level **8**

Materials: Paper and pencil, research sources – history book, Internet

Description: Have your child keep a diary from the perspective of a person working with Thomas Jefferson. What did Mr. Jefferson do today? What are his plans for tomorrow? What things did he do today that might have a big impact on our lives in the future? Have him share his diary with you.

NATIONAL U.S. HISTORY STANDARD ERA 4, STANDARD 3
HISTORICAL THINKING STANDARD 3 B

Vote for Who?

Number of People: 2 Time: Hour+

Grade Level **8**

Materials:Paper and colored pencils or markers, research sources – history book, Internet

Description: Presidential elections are always interesting. Some of our most recent ones have been very close. Look back to the Lincoln-Douglas era. Have your child choose one of the candidates. Let him create campaign signs and slogans for his candidate. He'll need to know something about the candidates and the major issues of the day to get his slogans on target.

NATIONAL U.S. HISTORY STANDARD ERA 5, STANDARDS 1, 2, & 3
HISTORICAL THINKING STANDARDS 2 G & 4 A

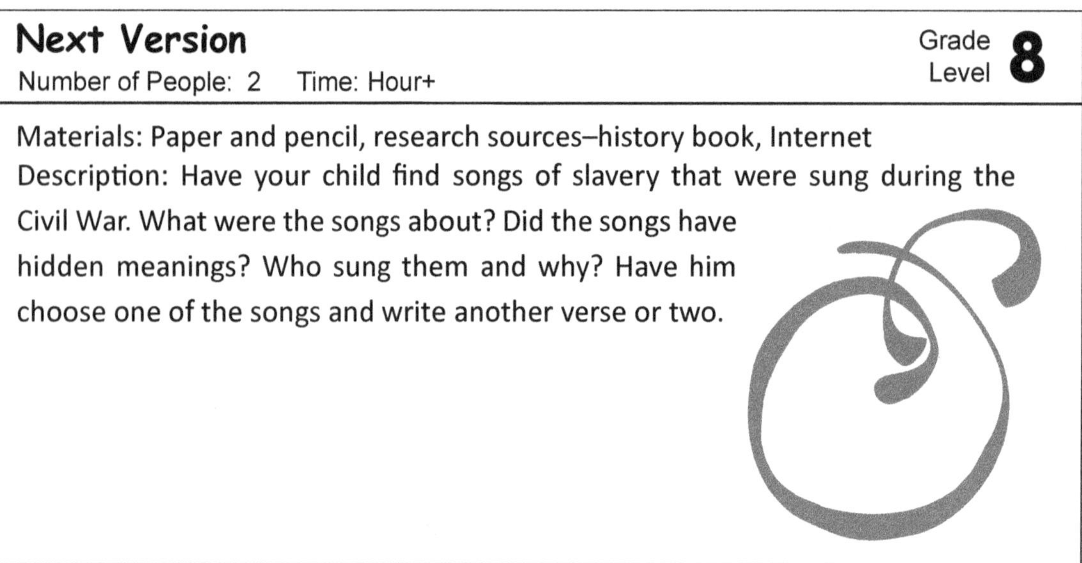

Next Version

Number of People: 2 Time: Hour+

Grade Level **8**

Materials: Paper and pencil, research sources–history book, Internet

Description: Have your child find songs of slavery that were sung during the Civil War. What were the songs about? Did the songs have hidden meanings? Who sung them and why? Have him choose one of the songs and write another verse or two.

NATIONAL U.S. HISTORY STANDARD ERA 5, STANDARDS 1, 2, & 3

HISTORICAL THINKING STANDARD 2 I

Historic Letter: Civil War

Number of People: 2+ Time: Hour+

Grade Level **8**

Materials: Paper and ink, research sources – history book, Internet

Description: Ask your child to write you a special letter. Tell him you'd like one from a Rebel at the end of the Civil War. What happened? Why was the war fought? Between whom? Over what? What is his Rebel opinion about the war? What were his reasons for joining the fight? Where is he now? Who is his hero? What were the results of this war? In his opinion, what brought about final peace?

NATIONAL U.S. HISTORY STANDARD ERA 5, STANDARDS 1, 2, & 3

HISTORICAL THINKING STANDARD 3 C & J

Famous Women

Number of People: 2 Time: 45 minutes

Grade Level **8**

Materials: Paper and pencil, research sources – history book, Internet

Description: Encourage your child to choose a famous woman from history to research. He could choose a woman active in the woman's suffrage movement. Take a look at Elizabeth Cady Stanton, Lucretia Mott, or Susan B. Anthony. Let him search the Internet and the library for information. Next have him choose a modern woman he looks up to and compare. Are there women today with similar careers and philosophies? Let him tell you how women's lives today are similar and how they are different when compared to the famous women of our past.

NATIONAL U.S. HISTORY STANDARD ERA 5, STANDARD 2, ERA 3, STANDARD 2
HISTORICAL THINKING STANDARD 4 A & B

What we learned today...

High Tech

Number of People: 2 Time: Hour+

Grade Level **8**

Materials: Paper and colored pencils, research sources – history book, Internet

Description: In the Industrial Revolution there were many new discoveries, inventions, and technologies. Have your child choose one and create an advertisement. He can check out Thomas Edison, Alexander Graham Bell, or the Wright Brothers for some ideas. Have him write the advertisement and make a poster. He can sell you the newest invention from the late 1800s by explaining its importance to your household today.

NATIONAL U.S. HISTORY STANDARD ERA 6, STANDARDS 1, 2, 3 & 4
HISTORICAL THINKING STANDARD 2 I & 4 B

Labor Union Issues

Number of People: 2 Time: 30 Minutes

Grade Level 

Materials: Paper, colored pencils or markers

Description: Have your child create a flyer to distribute among his family members regarding an issue that's important to him. Perhaps they no longer want to take out the trash or do the dishes. Management is forcing them to do so. The flyer should indicate why this is such an important issue and what should be done. Since I'm certain there will be negotiations, let him know what the consequences might be if his persuasive techniques succeed. If it's a legitimate request, honor it. If it means trash up to your eyebrows, you may not want to. Remember, there's usually a reasonable compromise.

NATIONAL U.S. HISTORY STANDARD ERA 9, STANDARD 4, ERA 10, STANDARD
HISTORICAL THINKING STANDARD 2 B

What we learned today...

Create your own playbook activities!

History

Number of People: Time:

Grade Level

Materials:

Description:

U.S. HISTORY LEARNING STANDARDS

HISTORICAL THINKING STANDARDS

History

Number of People: Time:

Grade Level

Materials:

Description:

U.S. HISTORY LEARNING STANDARDS

HISTORICAL THINKING STANDARDS

Create your own playbook activities!

History Number of People: Time:	Grade Level
Materials: Description:	

U.S. HISTORY LEARNING STANDARDS

HISTORICAL THINKING STANDARDS

History Number of People: Time:	Grade Level
Materials: Description:	

U.S. HISTORY LEARNING STANDARDS

HISTORICAL THINKING STANDARDS

INDEX

Parent Playbooks Order Form

Grade	# of Copies	Per Copy	Total
Pre-Sch	_______	$19.95	_______
K-2	_______	$19.95	_______
3-5	_______	$19.95	_______
6-8	_______	$19.95	_______
Subtotal			_______
Tax		x	_______
Total with tax			_______
Postage / Handling $3.00/bk			_______
Total			_______

Name: ____

Address: ______________________________________

City: ____________________ St: ____ Zip: __________

Phone:__________________ Fax: _________________

Email: ____

Check or money order #: ______________

Purchase Order # ____________________

Mail to:
Engage! Press
2485 Notre Dame Blvd 370-170
Chico, CA 95928

Or by Fax or Email:
Fax: 530-899-8423
www.familyfriendlyschools.com

Parent Playbooks Activities Form

I have a favorite activity to include in an upcoming parent playbook. It's in the area of:

- [ ] English/Language Arts
- [ ] Math
- [ ] Science
- [ ] Social Studies

Grade Level: Preschool K-2 3-5 6-8 9-12

Your Name: ______________________________

Address: ______________________________

City: ____________________ St: ____ Zip: __________

Email: ______________________________

School child attends: ______________________________

Location: ______________________________

Mail to:
Engage! Press
2485 Notre Dame Blvd 370-170
Chico, CA 95928

Or by Fax or Email:
Fax: 530-899-8423
www.familyfriendlyschools.com

Create your own playbook activity

Number of People:	Time:	Grade Level

Materials:

Description:

www.ingramcontent.com/pod-product-compliance
Lightning Source LLC
Chambersburg PA
CBHW080512110426
42742CB00017B/3084

9780990633549